The
EXETER
BOOK

Artefacts from Exeter past and present

The EXETER

BOOK

A PICTORIAL STUDY

PUBLISHED BY DEVON BOOKS
IN ASSOCIATION WITH EXETER CITY COUNCIL

First published in Great Britain in 1992 by Devon Books

British Library Cataloguing in Publication Data
Butler, Simon, 1950–
The Exeter Book
I. Title
942.356

ISBN 0 86114 871 1

THE EXETER BOOK

This book was conceived and produced by Devon Books and Exeter City Council under its Director of Planning, Colin Day. The text, layout and design of the work was completed by John Clark, Simon Butler and Andy Jones.

The Exeter Book has been produced entirely by companies within the city.

ACKNOWLEDGEMENTS

The Publishers and Exeter City Council particularly wish to thank the following individuals who kindly contributed to the publication of this work: John Allen, Jane Baker, Chris Henderson, and the staff of the Royal Albert Memorial Museum, Exeter; Peter Thomas; and the various companies and organisations who provided essential help, including Peninsular Repro, and BPCC Wheatons Ltd.

The photographs were provided by Peter Thomas; Ashley Thompson; John Risdon; John Clark; Andy Jones; Delphine Jones; David Garner; Valerie Allilouev; Dick Cooke and Graham Ward. Other photographs were provided by HMSO; South West Water; the National Rivers Authority; Devon Record Office; The West Country Studies Library; Devon Books; The Devon & Exeter Institution; Exeter City Council; Exeter University; The Royal Mail; The City Councils of Rennes, Bad Homburg and Terracina; and the organisations and companies who feature in the book.

Designed by Andy Jones
Topics Visual Information
397 Topsham Road, Exeter EX2 6HD
Tel: 0392 876800

DEVON BOOKS
Official Publisher to Devon County Council

Sales and general enquiries:
1 Chinon Court, Lower Moor Way, Tiverton EX16 6SS
Tel: 0884 243242   Fax: 0884 243325

Production Office:
397 Topsham Road, Exeter EX2 6HD
Tel: 0392 873215

Typesetting by ICON, Exeter

CONTENTS

A summer's day in the Cathedral Close.

INTRODUCTION

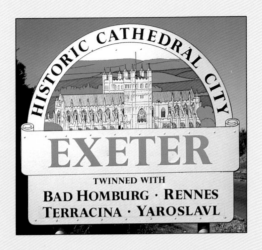

T he task of producing a single book that captures the essential nature of a city as varied as Exeter is not an easy one. To relate the events of two thousand years of the city's history, even in the briefest form, would require whole volumes. By using photographs it has been possible to provide a 'picture in time' of the city as it has developed over the centuries up to the present day.

Whether the reader is a visitor to Exeter, or is 'born and bred' it is hoped that *The Exeter Book* will give pleasure and some surprise glimpses of our splendid city.

A distant view of the city across rolling countryside. Exeter still enjoys the 'city in the country' image as suggested by Richard Ford the nineteenth century writer: "This Exeter is quite a capital, abounding in all that London has except its fog and smoke".

EXETER
— IN —
CONTEXT

An early nineteenth century view from the
north-west.

EXETER
— IN —
CONTEXT

T he special quality of Exeter is in no small measure due to its location at the heart of the South West peninsula. The following pages put the city in the context of the surrounding countryside, rich in scenic beauty and steeped in history.

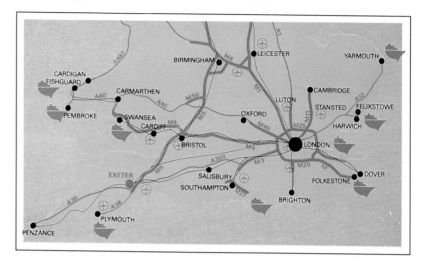

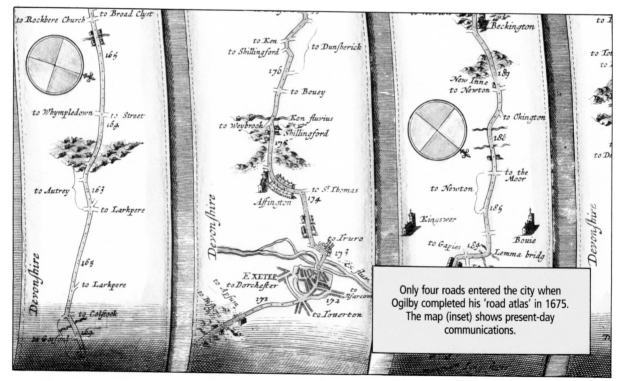

Only four roads entered the city when Ogilby completed his 'road atlas' in 1675. The map (inset) shows present-day communications.

2

The M5 crosses the River Exe at Topsham.

Exeter airport serves a variety of long- and short-haul operators, with daily flights to the capital.

Just over two hours from Paddington, the 125 High Speed Train enters Exeter St David's.

A commuter train approaches the city alongside the Exe estuary.

Bennett's Cross.

Haytor.

Postbridge.

Dartmoor – 95 000 hectares of National Park on Exeter's doorstep provides instant access to wide open spaces.

The mysterious Beer-stone quarry.

The delights of the seaside are only a short distance from the city.

Beer Cliffs overlooking the Channel. The white Beer stone and the honey-coloured stone from nearby Salcombe Regis were used to build the Cathedral. Worked until the last century, the quarries have since provided small quantities of stone for Cathedral repairs. The Guildhall portico is also constructed from this stone.

To the south-west of the city the Haldon Hills (left) dominate the skyline and Haldon Belvedere (above) is a famous landmark. The tower is an eighteenth-century memorial to General Stringer Lawrence, built by his friend Sir Robert Palk. Together they shared adventure with the East India Company. They now lie buried in nearby Dunchideock churchyard.

The River Exe widens as it flows across Exminster Marshes towards Exmouth and the sea. Running alongside the river is the Exeter Canal with its popular lockside inns.

Many great houses were built close to Exeter in the eighteenth and nineteenth centuries, among them Powderham Castle – home of the Earls of Devonshire – built on the site of an earlier fortified house. Here fallow deer still roam in the deer park.

Killerton House, home of the Acland family, is managed by the National Trust. Its superb gardens and woodland attract thousands of visitors.

Fallow deer at Powderham.

Killerton House.

Powderham Castle *c.* 1830.

A distant view of Topsham across the estuary.

EXETER'S VILLAGES

AND SUBURBS

Countess Wear.

Pennsylvania Park.

M any of the villages surrounding Exeter have been absorbed by the city, although some of them retain their earlier character.

Alphington – still retains an air of its quiet past and independence. Solid traditional houses speak of a rural gentry engaged in agricultural pursuits. Here was held the largest horse fair in the county. There is little sign now of Alphington Halt on the Exeter-Newton Abbot branch line, closed in 1958.

Pinhoe – is now a suburb of Exeter although aspects of the former village are still evident. There is a legend that the Danes defeated an Anglo-Saxon army here despite the efforts of a local priest who rode into the city to collect more arrows for the Saxon army. The imposing Pinbrook House is said to be one of the first brick buildings in the city.

St Thomas – covered a large area to the west of the River Exe. Here remains the portal of the county debtors' prison. Before the flood relief scheme came into being St Thomas suffered serious flooding on many occasions.

St David's – The original North Gate of the city once overlooked this small settlement across the Longbrook Valley. A number of interesting buildings stand close to the church of St David. The late eighteenth-century 'Walnut House' is one of the city's most attractive buildings from that period.

Heavitree – grew to become the largest and most important of the city parishes. Here, far from the city walls, condemned prisoners and heretics met their fate, the last being Thomas Benet in 1531, who was burnt at the stake. Although little of the pattern of the original 'village' is now apparent there are many interesting buildings. Heavitree stone, a warm red sandstone, was quarried here and is used in many of the city's buildings.

Pennsylvania – Named after the Quaker William Penn's New World community of the same name, this suburb began life as a terrace of six houses in 1818. The area still retains an air of exclusivity on the hills overlooking the city, with many fine residential buildings, including Pennsylvania Park.

St Leonard's – Once the smallest rural parish in Devon, developed in the Regency period as a suburban haven for the middle classes. It remains a desirable place to live and fine residential buildings abound.

Countess Wear – Set alongside the river, picturesque cottages hint at the hamlet's rural past. The area was important for its lime kilns and shipbuilding, and Glasshouse Lane is so called after an early eighteenth century glassworks.

Exwick – Once surrounded by rolling farmland, Exwick has grown into one of the city's largest suburbs, but one or two quiet corners remain.

Whipton – has changed much since Wippa, a Saxon farmer, first tilled the soil here. Houses now stand on the once fertile hills.

Debtors' prison, St Thomas.

St. David's

The village cross, Alphington.

Pinbrook House, Pinhoe.

Exwick.

The River Exe at Bickleigh.

The source of the Exe, Exmoor.

THE
RIVER EXE

Isca, a 'river full of fish', was the name given by the Romans to their settlement. Salmon are still caught in the Exe – less plentiful than in times past – and fishing is now carefully controlled by the National Rivers Authority.

Avocets, one of the success stories of bird protection, are welcome visitors to the Exe estuary. Rarer species such as Brent Geese and Bar-tailed Godwit are among the thousands of wintering birds.

Oystercatchers (right) are a common sight on the estuary mudflats.

The Exe estuary provides many sea-birds and waders with a protected haven, safe from all but the eyes and cameras of thousands of birdwatchers.

Netting salmon on the estuary (below). Brown trout (inset).

The Exe estuary.

TOPSHAM

Ferry Road.

The Bridge Inn.

Topsham was the most important port on the River Exe and served as the major port for the city with goods being taken by road to and from Exeter.

Though the opening of the Exeter Canal in 1566 transferred some trade to Exeter, Topsham remained the principal port throughout Exeter's heyday in the woollen trade. It was also chiefly involved in the fishing trade sending boats to the Newfoundland Banks for cod. Its prosperity through two centuries from 1600 onwards is evident in the fine buildings that remain, particularly some splendid merchants' houses.

In the Strand are the exceptionally fine 'Dutch' houses which were built c. 1680-1725 by Topsham merchants from bricks brought as ballast, and influenced by the architecture of Holland.

The waterfront area today gives little idea of the original port. Wharfs, limekilns and boatyards once lined the riverside where ropemaking and nailmaking were important trades. Topsham's Museum provides a fascinating account of the town's place in history.

Topsham is greatly favoured as a place to live, and as a centre for more leisurely maritime activities. It is this, coupled with splendid views across the estuary, that make Topsham such

a popular place – and yet full of unexpected quiet corners.

Topsham has had any number of notable inns many of them reflecting the seafaring connections of the town: the Salutation, the Globe, the Passage House, the Steam Packet, the Lighter, the Lord Nelson and the Bridge Inn.

During his progress through the West of England in 1680, the Duke of Monmouth visited Topsham. He is said to have addressed the townspeople from an open bay window at No. 9 Monmouth Street, formerly the Duke of Monmouth Inn. Later that decade, in 1688, William of Orange landed at Brixham, challenging the Kingship of James II. William rode overland to Exeter but his baggage was taken by sea to Topsham. William of Orange House in the Strand bears his name to this day.

Higher Shapter Street (above).

No. 9 Monmouth Street (above right) from which the Duke made his address to the people of Topsham.

Strand (below).

The Steam Packet

The Exe narrows on its approach from the city to the estuary, confined within manmade banks of the Quay and the flood relief scheme. Over the centuries weirs have been constructed to control the flow of the river. The famous traveller, Celia Fiennes, writing in 1698, records men spearing leaping salmon on the weirs above Exe Bridge.

The city viewed from the canal (above); contrast this with the view in John Gendall's (1789-1865) painting. Though methods of transport have changed, in some ways the scene has remained remarkably unchanged in over a hundred years.

Exeter from the Canal Basin (Gendall).

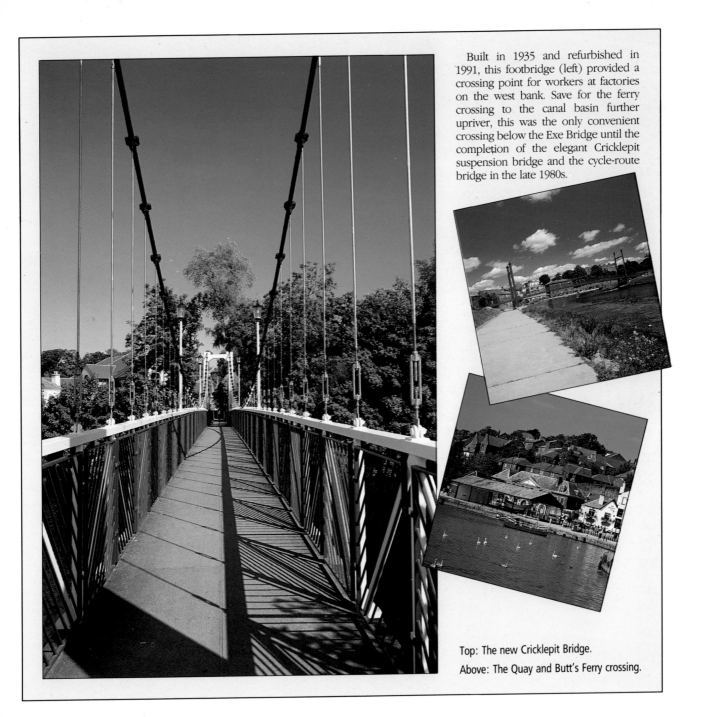

Built in 1935 and refurbished in 1991, this footbridge (left) provided a crossing point for workers at factories on the west bank. Save for the ferry crossing to the canal basin further upriver, this was the only convenient crossing below the Exe Bridge until the completion of the elegant Cricklepit suspension bridge and the cycle-route bridge in the late 1980s.

Top: The new Cricklepit Bridge.

Above: The Quay and Butt's Ferry crossing.

The Exeter Ship
CANAL

EXETER   Canal Stages

1566

1675

1827

Development of the Exeter Ship Canal

Turf Locks

The passage of shipping into the city was always hampered by the shallowness of the river and goods were usually off-loaded at Topsham. In medieval times various weirs were constructed on the river and these further obstructed the free flow of river traffic. In 1564 John Trew cut a 2 kilometre channel to bypass the weirs and to allow boats of 16 tonnes up to the city quays. Trew's canal, 5 metres wide and only 1 metre in depth, incorporated the first use of pound locks in this country. Trew's Weir was constructed to provide a sufficient depth of water in the canal.

In 1676 the canal was extended to Topsham and a large transhipment basin was built near the entrance. Between 1698 and 1701 the canal was straightened and enlarged to 15 metres wide and 2.5 metres in depth in order to admit coasting vessels of up to 150 tonnes. A new lock – Double Locks, – was built to replace three others.

From 1821 onwards many other improvements were carried out under James Green. He raised the banks and extended the canal to Turf Locks so that sea-going craft could reach it at all states of the tide. In 1827 the Canal Basin was opened as an alternative to vessels using the riverside quays. This took vessels of up to 400 tonnes and 3 metres draught.

The canal we see today – 3.5 kilometres in length – results from Green's engineering. It is used now as a major recreational facility and the Basin is the home of the internationally famous Maritime Museum.

On each of the major locks stand The Turf Locks Hotel and the Double Locks – once catering for the canal trade – now favourite stopping places en route for walkers and those taking canal trips.

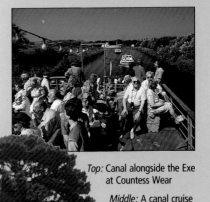

Top: Canal alongside the Exe at Countess Wear

Middle: A canal cruise

Left: Double Locks

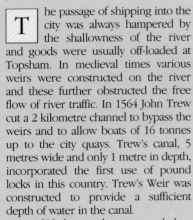

The
CUSTOM
HOUSE

'*ust by this key [quay] is the Custome house, an open space below with rows of pillars which they lay in goods just as its unladen out of the ships ....*' Celia Fiennes c. 1698.

Built in 1681, the Custom House on the Quay reflects Exeter's historical importance as a centre of trade. It was one of the first brick buildings in Exeter. The front was originally colonnaded with leaded windows above the arcading like those which can still be seen at the rear. Of particular note are the plasterwork ceilings and the staircase with heavy balusters.

At the time it was built Exeter was approaching its zenith as a commercial and industrial city, one of the foremost in England. Merchants were self-confident in the knowledge that the demand for Devon serges had never been greater – and that Exeter and Topsham daily bustled with shipping carrying goods to and from Europe and, increasingly, to the Far East. Importers of sugar, rice, coffee, tea and wine played a prominent role in the commercial and political life of the city.

All this trade had to pass through the City's Custom House and its bonded stores on the quay. Celia Fiennes describes '*a large room full of desks and little partitions for the writers and accountants, it was full of books and files of paper...*'

Close to the Custom House stands the Wharfinger's Office, built in 1778, from where the quayside traffic was controlled. Nearby, under the canopy of the transit sheds, is the King's Beam, used by Customs Officers for suspending their weighing scales. The cast-iron beam was made by Bodleys of Exeter in 1838.

Bolts of cloth, ready for export, were carefully weighed and each was stamped using a tillet block.

In the days of smugglers the Custom and Excise Officers at Exeter manned a cutter, the *Alarm*, which had a crew of 21. Contraband was a major business and smugglers, including the infamous Jack Rattenbury of Beer, posed major headaches for the authorities. Rattenbury was detained for a time at His Majesty's Pleasure in Exeter Gaol.

The King's Beam under the transit shed

Tillet Block
Jack Rattenbury

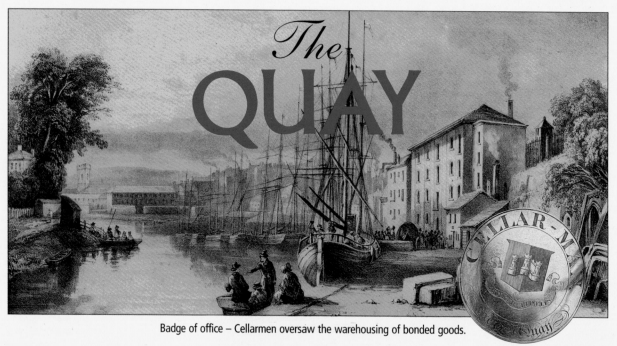

The QUAY

Badge of office – Cellarmen oversaw the warehousing of bonded goods.

The Quay was originally a landing area for off-loading goods, with sea-going ships coming upriver only as far as Topsham. Wattle hurdles formed the quaysides until the late sixteenth century when a stone quay was built.

The construction of the canal at the end of the sixteenth century brought about further improvements and in the seventeenth century the Custom House and a new 'Quay House' were built. The latter building now houses an interpretation centre.

From the late nineteenth century the area declined, warehouses and other buildings falling into disrepair as maritime trade ceased. (See 'Riverside Revival'.)

The drawings below show the development of the Quay.

1605: The Watergate to the rear, the Little Island, lime kiln, crane and Quay House.

1690: The Custom House and Quay House with its dock *(illustrations by Jane Brayne)*.

1720: Following improvements to the Canal, sea-going ships could now reach the Quay.

The EXE BRIDGES

The medieval bridge *(illustrations by Graham Moores)*.

The stone bridge of 1790.

The steel bridge of 1905.

The modern bridge.

I n choosing the site for their fort, the Romans selected the lowest fording point on the River Exe. It is possible that they built a timber bridge here but the first stone bridge was constructed at the end of the twelfth century, replacing a footbridge. This magnificent multi-arched bridge remained in use until 1790 and it can still be seen – now about half the original length.

The replacement bridge was much shorter in length, three arches spanning the river from Cowick Street to New Bridge Street. This too was replaced, in 1905, by an elegent steel bridge designed to carry electric trams. Two concrete bridges took its place in 1972.

Top left: The steel bridge before demolition in 1972.
Top right: Remains of the medieval bridge today.
Inset: A lamp standard from the 1905 bridge, now on the Quay.

EXETER IN FLOOD

Floods in St Thomas

Part of the flood relief scheme

T he River Exe in times of flood has proved a wild and unpredictable threat to the city. To watch the river on a bright summer day, gently gliding under the city's bridges, it is difficult to believe the ferocity and power it can wield.

The photographs on these pages show scenes from the flooding of the city in the past – now no longer the threat it was due to the elaborate flood-prevention measures taken in the late 60s and early 70s.

The major flood-prevention work has taken place above the Exe Bridges where a huge catchment scheme channels flood water safely through the vulnerable areas of the city.

Flood waters sweep beneath Exe Bridge

FIRE!

(Top) Exeter's Fire Brigade *c.* 1900. (Centre) Identifying bodies following the theatre fire. (Bottom) The rebuilt Theatre Royal, demolished 1962

A great disaster befell the city on 5 September 1887. During a performance of *Romany Rye*, fire broke out in the Theatre Royal in Longbrook Street. Within seconds the fire caught hold and, panic stricken, men and women fought to escape the flames. Next morning 186 bodies were recovered from the burnt-out building. The fire directly resulted in an Act of Parliament regulating safety in theatres throughout the country.

Athelstan's Tower. Named after the King who ordered the rebuilding of the city walls in the tenth century. In fact the present tower is from the late fourteenth or early fifteenth century.

THE
CITY IN HISTORY

The courtyard of the Bishop of Crediton's House,
Cathedral Close.

THE
ROMANS
(ISCA DUMNONIORUM)

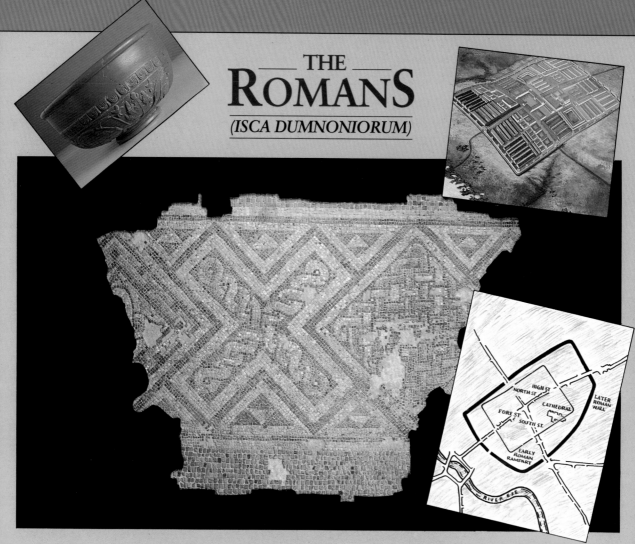

During almost four centuries of Roman occupation the city became a regional centre for trade and culture as many archaeological discoveries confirm. An everyday reminder of the Roman presence is the city wall, built c. AD 200, the line of which has remained unchanged since Roman times, with several sections of Roman masonry visible.

This plan (lower right) shows the location and size of the original Roman fortress at *Isca* c. AD 70, and the city wall is shown surrounding the later 'civil' settlement.

Excavations on the site of the Legionary bath-house began in 1971 in the Cathedral Close. The findings were beyond all expectations: parts of the hypocaust of the original military bath-house and the later basilica were uncovered.

A Roman mosaic pavement was uncovered in 1989 at the site of St Catherine's Almshouses (above centre).

The Romans occupied *Isca* until the withdrawal of the legions in the fifth century. (Top left) Samian bowl AD 200.

A reconstruction of the Roman bath house (caldarium)

Viewing the Roman mosaic.

Tile decorations
from the baths.

Excavating in Cathedral Close, 1971.

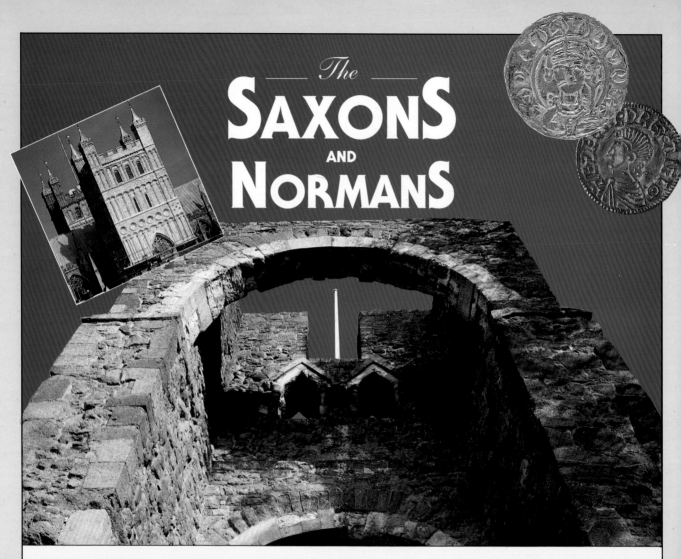

The
SAXONS
AND
NORMANS

S axon resistance in Exeter continued after the Norman victory at Hastings and, in 1068, William arrived to besiege the city. For eighteen days the defenders fought off daily attacks and eventually an honourable surrender was agreed.

The lasting presence of the Normans can be seen in many parts of the city but nowhere more spectacularly than in the twin towers of the Cathedral.

To protect himself against further Saxon unrest William ordered that Rougemont Castle be built. The gatehouse, an early example of Norman military engineering, still stands at the top of Castle Street.

Perhaps William's greatest legacy is the Domesday Book. The Exeter Book *(Liber Exoniensis)*, covering the south-western counties, appears to be an early draft of the Exchequer Domesday and thus forms a vital part of the nation's historical heritage.

Norman Font.

"Land of the Bishop of Exeter – The Bishop of Exeter has in the City 1 church which pays 1 silver mark. 47 houses pay 10s 10d; 2 houses have been destroyed by fire ..." (entry from the Exon. Domesday).

The Benedictine Priory of St Nicholas was founded around 1080. Following the dissolution of the Monasteries by Henry VIII in 1536 most of the building was demolished except for the north and west wings. Above is shown the Priory Hall built above the vaulted Norman undercroft.

THE EXETER BOOK

This fascinating Anglo-Saxon work was left to the Cathedral Library by Bishop Leofric when he died in 1072. Only four great miscellanies of Old English poetry survive and this is one of them. The ninety-six riddles in the book constitute a rare glimpse of the Anglo-Saxon world:

I am told a certain object grows in the corner, rises and expands, throws up a crust. A proud wife carried off that boneless wonder, the daughter of a king covered that swollen thing with a cloth.

What am I?*

The CITY WALL

The Roman wall.

East Gate by John Hayman.

SITE OF WEST GATE SUCCESSFULLY DEFENDED AGAINST THE REBEL ATTACKS IN 1549 WILLIAM PRINCE OF ORANGE WITH HIS ARMY ENTERED THE CITY IN 1688 THROUGH THIS GATE WHICH WAS REMOVED IN 1815.

East Gate, as it appeared in the sixteenth century.

A PLAN of ROUGEMONT CASTLE, as describ'd by LELAND, in the 16th Century.

Northernhay

City Wall

200 Yards

Foſſe

Foſſe

Counterſcarp.

County Gaol.

City Wall

References

1. Seſſions-houſe. 2. Donjon.
3. A cover'd Flight of Steps. that
led to the top of the Donjon.
4. Sally Port, with a cover'd way
to the Drawbridge 5.
6. Subterraneous paſſage to ditch
7. Guard-houſe.
8. An ancient Gateway walled up.
9. Towers or Baſtions.
10. Entrance from the City flank'd
by a cover'd way that led to the

Drawbridge 11.
12. A machiolated Gateway: the ori
ginal entrance, altered by the
Norman Conqueror.
13. House of the Caſtellan.
14. Chapel, olim Collegiate,
dedicated to the Virgin Mary.
15. Armoury.
16. A deep Well.
17. Tower on the City wall.

10 20 30 40 50
Scale of Yards.

32

E arly maps show the city nestling within the encircling walls and even today practically the whole circuit can be followed. Surviving Roman masonry in typical herringbone pattern can be seen, notably near the gateway between Rougemont and Northernhay Gardens.

It seems likely that the walls fell into disrepair after the Romans left Britain. The Danes attacked the city in AD 876 and again in 1003, although on the second occasion they relied on the treachery of the City Reeve to allow them in through an opened gate.

The Norman invasion saw Saxon resistance in the West centred on Exeter. As described earlier in this book, the city surrendered to William only after an eighteen day siege.

In 1136, Baldwin de Redvers, in support of Queen Matilda, occupied Rougemont Castle. King Stephen laid siege and, when first the water and then supplies of wine ran out, the Castle was surrendered.

The walls withstood further attack in 1497 when the imposter Perkin Warbeck led his followers to the city gates.

Exeter's first historian John Hooker (or Hoker) was present during the Western Rebellion of 1549 when, in a month-long siege, an attempt was made by the rebels to burn the West and South Gates. They were repelled: *'the great porte peces were chardged with greate bags of flynte stones and hayle shote and as they were approaching vnto the gate the gate would be secretilie opened and the said porte peces dyscharged...'*

A later historian (Jenkins – *History of Exeter*, 1806) recalled seeing one of these cannon lying near the East Gate *'twelve feet in length and twelve inches in diameter at the mouth'*.

It was Mayor Blackaller who led the citizens to the walls overlooking the rebel throng, exchanging defiant remarks with their leaders. A two-month siege ended when the King's forces

bloodily defeated the rebels at Fenny Bridges on the Honiton road.

The four major gates of the city were built up into massive bastions, each heavily defended. Gatekeepers were responsible each night for closing the gates and securing them, a highly regarded position. In 1760 the keeper of the West Gate drew an annual salary of £1.1s.

As the city gates were no longer needed for defence and hindered the free flow of traffic, the Chamber of Exeter took steps towards their demolition. The North Gate was torn down in 1769, the East Gate removed in 1784, the South Gate, West Gate and Watergate all went in 1819.

Excavations prior to new building in South Street in 1964 revealed the site of the Roman gate near South Gate.

In 1814 an elegant footbridge was erected across a 'cut' in the wall on the order of Mayor Burnet Patch (below left).

The 'New Cut' footbridge.

The Cathedral Gates

The Close of the Middle Ages was an area surrounding the Cathedral, separating Church from City. It is said the walls and gates were constructed following the murder of Walter de Lechlade in the thirteenth century. Seven gates allowed access to the Close, each joined by walls which themselves linked to the city walls. Broad Gate was the main entrance (removed 1825), the site of which is today marked by posts.

Wynard's Almshouses.

MEDIEVAL
EXETER

Bowhill House.

I n medieval times Exeter was a major ecclesiastical centre. Almost one-third of the land within the city walls belonged to the Church. In addition to the Cathedral there were 32 parish churches, seven monasteries and several chapels and hospitals. Improvements such as the building of the Exe Bridge, the construction of the Underground Passages to bring water to the city, and extensive repairs to the city wall were undertaken.

Wynard's Almshouses (above) in Magdalen Street. Built in 1453 and restored in 1863, they form one of the most evocative pieces of medieval Exeter. Amongst the property with which William Wynard endowed the

almshouses was the Blue Boar Inn in South Street, now the White Hart.

St Mary Steps (below, left). On the red sandstone tower of this fifteenth century church is the famous Matthew the Miller clock whose figures strike the hour. It is said the clock was named after a local miller who regulated his life with such clockwork precision that his neighbours used him as a living timepiece.

The extraordinary 'House That Moved' (below). In 1961, in order to make way for the inner bypass, this sixteenth-century timber house was moved lock, shop and cockloft, to its present location. Originally a tradesman's house, with a shop on the ground floor, it had a small hall on the

first floor, a second floor chamber, and cockloft above.

Having undergone extensive and painstaking conservation of its fabric, Bowhill House (above) was recently opened to the public. It was built c. 1500 on Dunsford Hill in St Thomas by Roger Holland, Recorder of the City and an MP. Of particular interest is the joinery of the screens and roof.

Stepcote Hill (below) echoes with the footfalls of Exeter's past. Steps run up each side of the street for pedestrians, with a cobbled packhorse way in the centre. The street name comes from the Old English word for 'Steep'. In former times it was known as 'Mule Steps Hill' and an open drain ran down its centre.

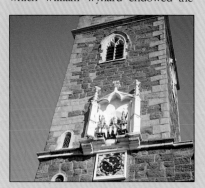
St Mary Steps Church.

The 'House That Moved'.

Stepcote Hill.

Lilly Wotton, an Exeter water seller.

LIFE
—TO THE—
CITY

The Underground Passages.

One of the reasons the Romans chose the site of Exeter was its plentiful water supply. Throughout the city their wood-lined wells have been found and excavated. Traces of an aqueduct were discovered in the High Street in 1980, which also supplied the Bath House located in the present-day Cathedral Close.

The most famous of Exeter's wells was Sidwell. The legend, possibly of pre-Christian origin, tells of Sidwella, an innocent maiden, who was murdered by her stepmother. Reapers working in the fields nearby were persuaded to cut off her head and where it fell a clear spring of water gushed from the earth. A church dedicated to St Sidwell stands outside the site of the former East Gate

The Great Conduit at Carfax brought water to the city centre at the junction of High Street and South Street.

and at the spring there many miracles are said to have occurred.

The Cathedral clergy were responsible for developing water supplies during the medieval period and their greatest civic enterprise, Exeter's Underground Passages, still exist. A guided

tour through these superbly constructed subterranean tunnels is one of the highlights of a visit to the city. The earliest of these tunnels was cut in the twelfth century to carry water from St Sidwell's well to a conduit in the Close and many sections survive beneath the city streets, a tribute to the engineering skills of their builders.

St Sidwell.

The GUILDS

The Sheriff's Chain.

Exeter Guildhall.

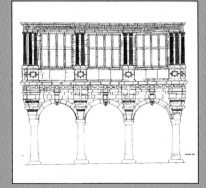

Original polychrome façade.

he Guilds were an important feature of late medieval life. In Exeter the various trades included barbers, cordwainers, apothecaries, butchers, as well as councillors, aldermen, and staffbearers, all of whom shared in the traditions and privileges of their respective craft.

A national statute of 1563 made apprenticeship compulsory for all craftsmen and the guilds controlled and collected payments from apprentices and their masters. Each had its own meeting house or guildhall from which the business of the guild was conducted and in which were held the records and regalia. Each held a celebration on its own feast day. Certain guilds became very powerful, particularly in matters of local politics and their influence lasted well into the nineteenth century.

Their power and influence in Exeter is represented by the magnificence of the Guildhall, rebuilt in 1468 with the fine portico added in 1592. During recent repairs many tiny fragments of colour were found on the stone of the portico, indicating that the façade was originally brightly coloured. The reconstruction (above, right) shows how the building may have looked in the late sixteenth century.

The interior is adorned with the arms of the city mayors, recorders, incorporated trades and benefactors. Many pictures of note hang here, including a portrait of Princess Henrietta Anne, sister of Charles II.

The hall of the Guildhall is one of the oldest municipal buildings in Britain. It houses a collection of silver presented to past Mayors and Sheriffs to mark their year in office, along with the city regalia, including a mourning sword presented by Edward IV.

Following the defeat of the Duke of Monmouth's ill-fated rebellion in 1685, the infamous Judge Jeffreys presided over grim sessions of the 'Bloody Assizes' in the Guildhall.

The Common Seal of the City of Exeter is thought to be the oldest civic seal in the country. Dating from the twelfth century it bears a symbolic representation of a city and its towered walls.

Exeter City Seal.

The Guildhall interior.

TUCKER'S HALL

The arms of the Tucker's Guild.

T he Company of Weavers, Fullers (Tuckers) and Shearmen were the most powerful of the Exeter Guilds. The Company is still in existence today. Tucker's Hall in Fore Street, built in 1471 is among the city's architectural treasures. The building fell into disrepair in the last century and the restoration included the complete rebuilding of the façade.

Visitors to Tucker's Hall will note particularly the panelling and carving, and the handsome furnishing and weaponry surviving from the days when the guild played its part in the defence of the city. The Company possesses a fine collection of silver but the most poignant exhibit is the fulling shears, weighing all of 12kg, a relic of the Company's founding industry.

The Beadle and tucking shears.

Sir Francis Drake.

TUDOR EXETER

Queen Elizabeth I.

B y the first quarter of the sixteenth-century Exeter was one of the greatest and richest towns in the Kingdom. Outside London, only Norwich, York, Bristol and Newcastle were larger.

Exeter became a great trading centre and famous Devon sea captains – Drake, Raleigh, Frobisher and Hawkins – were often seen in the city.

In 1531 scandal shook the city. In a statement nailed to the Cathedral doors, Thomas Benet, an Exeter schoolmaster, had denounced the Pope as the Antichrist. This act, for which Benet was burnt at the stake, heralded in the Reformation.

Not least among the great events of the period was the Prayer Book Rebellion of 1549 when ten thousand men besieged Exeter for more than a month. Ever loyal to the Tudors, Exeter held out.

Later in the century, responding to an even greater threat, the city armed and manned three ships against the Spanish Armada. In recognition of this Queen Elizabeth I suggested the city's motto *Semper Fidelis* – 'Ever Faithful'. Completed at the end of the sixteenth century, the building now known as Mol's Coffee House (right) in the Close provides a glimpse of Exeter's grandeur and wealth in late Tudor times.

Mol's Coffee House. The Dutch gable was added in the late nineteenth century.

Principal room of 229 High Street

In 1587 Hogenburg produced the first map of the city (above).

Apart from the shop window, the façade of this superb Tudor building (below left), Nos 41-42 High Street, has changed little since it was built in 1549. It is in fact a pair of gable-ended houses erected as a single structure. Discovered here during renovation in 1980 were some vivid wall paintings (above left), simple decorative stripes and friezes, with contrasting colouring to highlight carved beams – early Tudor wallpaper!

One of the most elaborate Tudor houses in Exeter was constructed on the corner of Gandy Street in 1584. The house was demolished in 1930 and it is believed that parts of the interior were acquired by William Randolph Hearst the American newspaper tycoon. Subsequently the principal room passed to the Nelson Atkin's Museum of Kansas City USA where it is now a prize exhibit. The room had a decorated plaster ceiling and impressive timber panelled walls surmounted by a carved frieze with animal heads and floral patterns. The elaborately carved fireplace and overmantel incorporated decorative motifs including fluted pilasters and the coat of arms of Elizabeth I – it must have been one of the finest fireplaces in Exeter at that time.

The CIVIL WAR

T he Civil War began in 1642. At Exeter the citizens were deeply divided in their loyalty, although on the whole Devon was more Parliamentarian that Royalist. Exeter remained for Parliament until the Royalist victory at the Battle of Stratton after which the city surrendered

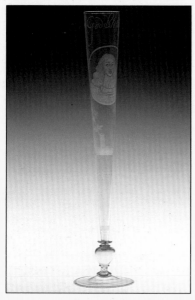

The 'Exeter' flute glass c.1660. Engraved with the inscription 'God Bless King Charles the Second'.

to Prince Maurice in 1643 and the whole of the West fell into Royalist hands.

Excavations in 1986 on the site of Hayes Barton in St Thomas revealed that the house had been used by the Royalists as a strongpoint overlooking Exe Bridge from which they could direct fire over the city. The fierceness of an assault from the city by 1100 Parliamentary soldiers in July 1643 is evidenced from a large quantity of musket balls found against the walls of the house.

Exeter's defences were considerably strengthened during this period. Gates and walls were repaired, batteries were mounted, and an external system of ditches and ramparts was created to provide defence in depth. Trees and houses near the wall were removed. During recent excavations in Magdalen Street parts of these defences were uncovered. They consisted of earth banks thrown up within musket shot of the city wall. They prevented cannon from being drawn up close to the walls and restricted their field of fire.

In the summer of 1644 Parliament took the offensive in the South West but the Earl of Essex suffered badly in Cornwall. Charles travelled to Exeter where his daughter was born at the Earl of Bedford's house in the city. Essex

was caught and defeated at Lostwithiel and the King's grip on the west was strengthened.

At Naseby, in 1645, the New Model Army crushingly defeated the Royalists. Fairfax and Cromwell turned their attention to the West and by October they were in Devon. One by one the country houses around Exeter were garrisoned by Parliamentary troops.

Five thousand Royalists sheltered within the city walls all that winter while Cromwell's soldiers cleared the rest of the County of their compatriots. In January 1646, at Poltimore House, Fairfax began to negotiate for the surrender of the city. Exeter capitulated in April and the war in the West was over.

The Parliamentarians then began the dismantling of much of the city's defenses and fortifications fearing the possibility of a Royalist rebellion in the city.

The Restoration was an occasion of great rejoicing and Charles II lost little time in visiting Exeter. He knighted the Mayor and presented the city with a portrait of his Exeter-born sister, Henrietta (right).

The citizens of Exeter gave Charles a magnificent silver table salt (right) which now forms one of the major pieces of the Crown Jewels.

East Gate during the siege of 1643 *(illustration: Piran Bishop).*

The GOLDEN AGE

1660–1720

B y 1660 the City was recovering from the effects of the Civil War and had entered its most prosperous age. The cloth trade remained the principal industry though the market had shifted from France to Holland.

Increased trade meant improvements to the port, not only to allow ease of exports, but to accommodate new imports of sugar from the West Indies, tobacco from America and wines from Spain and Portugal. On the back of such prosperity the city grew and thrived.

Much of Exeter's architectural heritage has been inevitably lost. This seventeenth century gallery at 38 North Street (below) was carefully surveyed before demolition in 1972 and much was learnt of its original structure and later development.

The 'Tudor House', Tudor Street (below) was built *c.*1660 and restored in the 1970s. Its slate hanging represents a particular style of decoration of which this is the best surviving example in Exeter.

Shop frontage, South Street.

Gallery at 38 North Street.

The 'Tudor House', Tudor Street.

Pinbrook House (detail, above), Pinhoe was built in 1679 by John Elwill, a successful local merchant.

(Top) Detail from the 'Tudor House'.

Bellair House.

Detail of late seventeenth-century plasterwork (right) from Bellair House, Exeter (now in the grounds of County Hall), designed on a martial theme.
Such plasterwork echoes the growing elegance in domestic decoration among the wealthier merchant classes. Exeter City Chamber accounts in 1681 record a payment of £35 to John Abbot of Frithelstock for plasterwork on the newly built Custom House. In 1689 the Chamber paid plasterer Thomas Lane £50 for the ceiling over the Apollo Room of the New Inn, High Street.

Detail of plasterwork (c.1700), originally from the Half Moon Inn on Exeter High Street, now in the Royal Albert Memorial Museum.

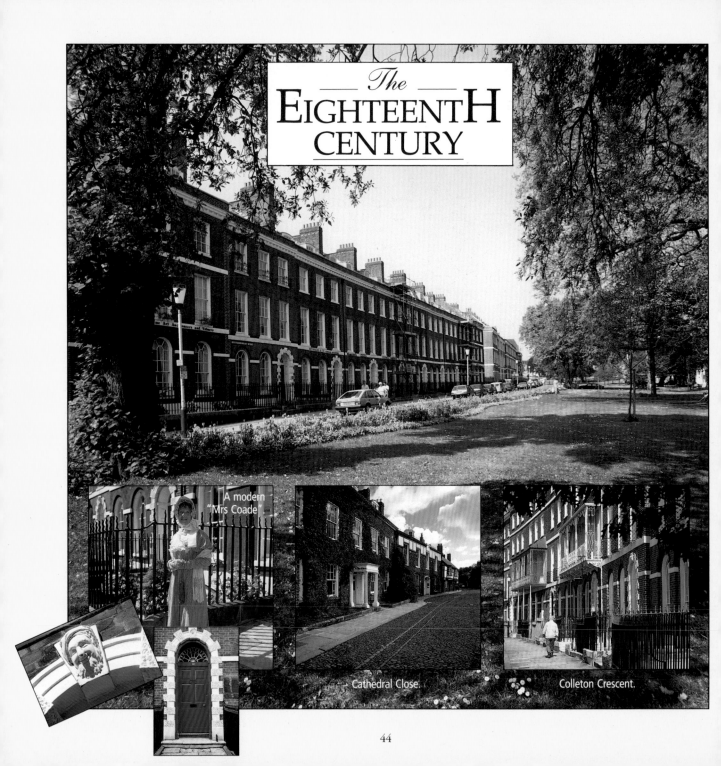

The EIGHTEENTH CENTURY

A modern "Mrs Coade"

Cathedral Close.

Colleton Crescent.

44

The Napoleonic Wars (1793-1815) put an end to European trade and, by the time peace was restored, the centre of textile manufacturing had moved to the Northern industrial towns. The Devon woollen industry collapsed.

The riverside acquired new industries: breweries, tanneries, a papermill and iron foundries. The old fulling mills were converted to new uses – such as the grinding of corn.

A bell foundry (below) in Paul Street had been operated in Exeter since 1625 by members of the Pennington family. This survived until 1720. They cast the bells for churches throughout Devon and for St Mary Steps Church in 1656. They also manufactured a wide range of domestic utensils such as skillets and cauldrons.

During the late eighteenth century the climate, amenities and scenery of Exeter attracted wealthy families from all over the country – a new middle class population with a substantial income to invest. The city began to develop as an administrative, financial and distributive centre and, in 1789 the Exeter Bank was the first of several to be established. During this period many attractive terraces and crescents were built to house the new middle classes.

(Top) Southernhay West – the principal builders of the period were Matthew Nosworthy and William Hooper. Nosworthy built many elegant terraces characterised by his use of Coade Stone dressings to door and window surrounds. (Bottom left and right) Georges Meeting – a Unitarian Church building completed in 1760. Recently renovated and converted into a shop and cafe restaurant, the building contains many fine features of the period.

"Tis full of gentry and good company, and yet full of trade and manufacture also. The serge market held here every week is very well worth a stranger seeing, and next to the Brigg market at Leeds in Yorkshire, is the greatest in England. The people assured me that at this market is generally sold from 60 to 70 to 80, and sometime a hundred thousand pounds."   Daniel Defoe 1724.

The NINETEENTH CENTURY

I n the first half of the nine-teenth century Exeter declined in national importance. By 1800 Exeter had fallen to fourteenth in size amongst provincial towns – by 1860 it was fortieth. However, during this time the population increased from 20000 to 50000. Engineering, iron founding, brewing, papermaking and printing industries developed. The canal was extended in 1825 and a new basin was opened in 1830.

An Exeter bank note (right).
Exeter's first bank (below).

(Top and above) Chichester Place
Southernhay East, built by
William Hooper and completed in 1825.

The young
Queen Victoria
looks down
over Queen
Street.

Along with the Underground Passages, the Catacombs (above) are one of the city's most intriguing sights. Built just below the city wall, and overlooking the gardens in the Longbrook Valley, they were designed in Egyptian style by Thomas Whitaker for public burials. Linked with tiers of underground chambers they allowed for an astonishing 22 000 bodies. In fact there were only a few interments.

The Victorians widened a number of Exeter's streets and imposed a new street, Queen Street (above right), on the medieval plan of the city. Begun in 1835, it was named after the new Queen and contains a group of imposing buildings including the Higher Market and the ornate Royal Albert Memorial Museum.

As the centre of 'polite society' in Exeter, Southernhay offered superior 'cold, hot, plunge, shower and medicated baths' (top right). An extraordinary edifice built in the fashionable neo-classical style in 1821, it was later demolished.

QUICKSILVER DAYS

A Royal Mail stamp.

The Toll House, Pinhoe.

Coaches stand outside the New London Inn c.1840.

T he first passenger coach service into Devon began in 1658, taking four days to journey from London to Exeter – at around three miles an·hour! Celia Fiennes described the appalling roads of the time 'the ways became so difficult that one could scarcely pass by each other...'

A stage coach from Exeter to Bath and Bristol ran in 1727 – but only in summer – and took three days to Bath. By 1764 the journey was down to two days, and twenty years later to 32 hours.

By 1828 the Devonport Mail was running to Exeter from London in less than 20 hours and, in a famous race between two coaches, the Quicksilver and Telegraph in 1835, the former reached Exeter in a little over 16 hours!

The effects of such a journey on the passengers especially those on the outside of the coach, can only·be imagined. The need for warm shelter and good food at the journey's end was paramount and Exeter had a large number of inns to cater for the weary traveller.

The New London, Royal Clarence, Globe, Half Moon, White Lion, Seven Stars, White Hart, and Crown and Sceptre are just a few names of hostelries recommended in guidebooks of the period.

Charles Dickens writing from the New London Inn in 1839 conjures a vivid picture of staying in such an establishment and its unlikely clientele: *'My quarters are excellent and the head waiter is such a waiter! . . . My first and only visitor came tonight. – A ruddy faced man in black with extracts from a feather bed all over him . . . I have not seen the proper waiter since and more than suspect I shall not recover from this blow. He was announced (by the waiter) as 'a person'. I expect my bill every minute.'*

TRAINS

The first steam locomotive entered Exeter on 1 May 1844 when the Bristol and Exeter Railway locomotive *Actaeon* arrived from Paddington after exactly five hours.

A few years later Isambard Kingdom Brunel extended the broad gauge South Devon Railway from Exeter to Plymouth, including a section of his ill-fated 'atmospheric' railway. Thousands attended the opening of Brunel's St David's station and a banquet was held in a converted goods shed.

St Thomas Station, also designed by Brunel (1846), and recently re-furbished, and Central Station (1933), are both still in use.

(Below) Iron Bridge, built, 1834.

TRAMS

Horse drawn trams were used in the city from late Victorian times and the first electric tram was introduced in 1905. Old photographs of the city show tramlines in all the main streets, with cumbersome poles carrying overhead wires. The last tram ran in 1931.

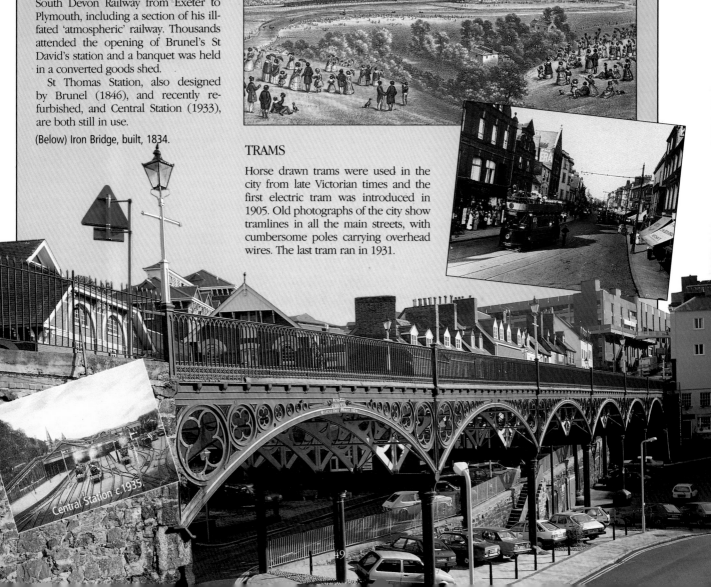

Central Station c.1935.

Nicholas Hilliard.

Exeter's
FAMOUS PEOPLE

John Veitch *(1752-1839)*, a Scotsman and horticulturalist, founded the internationally famous Veitch nurseries in Exeter. Working for Sir Thomas Acland, a tree nursery was established near Killerton and later with his son James, John Veitch developed the 25 acre nursery site at Mount Radford.

The business continued in the Veitch family until 1969 when it was sold to St Bridget Nurseries, also of Exeter.

Nicholas Hilliard *(c.1547-1619)* was the son of an Exeter Goldsmith. Though trained as a jeweller he became England's leading miniaturist painter with a reputation extending to France.

Sir Redvers Henry Buller *(c.1802-1884)*, whose statue stands near the junction of Queen Street and New North Road was the most famous soldier of his day. Awarded the Victoria Cross during the Zulu War he then earned greater fame for his relief of Ladysmith during the Boer campaign. A memorial and bust can be found in the Cathedral.

Charles Dickens (1812-1870) visited Exeter a number of times and is said to have frequented a coffee house, later the Wheaton Bookshop, in Fore Street. In Alphington stands the house Dickens bought for his parents. At the Turk's Head Dickens found the original of his Fat Boy for *Pickwick Papers*.

Sir Thomas Bodley *(1545-1613)* was born in Exeter and went on to found one of the world's greatest libraries, the Bodleian, in Oxford. A plaque to his memory can be seen at the corner of Gandy Street with the High Street.

Richard Hooker *(c.1554-1600)* was born in Heavitree. He is famous for his theological work *The Laws of Ecclesiasticall Politie*. His uncle John Hooker (alias Vowell) was first chamberlain of Exeter in 1555, and it was he who produced the earliest known map showing the Cathedral and Close where Richard's statue now stands.

Erecting Buller's statue, 1905.

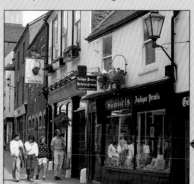

The Turk's Head, Waterbeer Street.

Richard Hooker and his present-day lookalike.

EXETER ARTISTS

William Gandy, whose family the Exeter street of that name commemorates, lived in Exeter until his death in 1729. He was among the foremost portrait painters of his day. **Thomas Patch** *(c.1725-82)* landscape and townscape painter spent most of his life in Italy. **John White Abbot** *(1763-1851)*. An apothecary and water-colourist, student of **Francis Towne** *(1740-1816)* who lived much of his life in Exeter. **John Wallace Tucker** *(1808-69)* painted in oil, sometimes on wood, Devon landscapes, as did **William** *(1826-93)* and his son **Frederick John Widgery** *(1861-1942)* whose Dartmoor landscapes dominate his work. Examples of the work of many of these artists can be seen at the Royal Albert Memorial Museum, Exeter.

One of most curious inhabitants of the city was **Joanna Southcott** *(1750-1814)*. Joanna gained national notoriety through her claims to be the future mother of the second Messiah, going as far to predict the date on which he would be born. Many people believed in her wild assertions and the South-cottians swore never to shave their beards which in consequence grew to enormous lengths.

In 1790 she was employed in the shop of an upholsterer in Exeter and, one day while sweeping the floor, she found a ring with the initials JS. This she took as a sign and her followers bought wax impressions of the ring and other charms for as much as a guinea apiece. She died in London but pockets of her followers lived in and around Exeter for many years after.

One of the most unwelcome visitors to the city was the **Duke of Monmouth** in 1680. Sir William Courtenay entertained him at the Deanery but, it is said, the civic authorities ignored him and the Cathedral bells remained silent.

Matthew Locke *(c.1630-1677)*, born in Exeter, become a chorister at the Cathedral (where he cut his name in the stone of the organ screen!). Later he was at the forefront of English musical composition as 'Composer in Ordinary' to the King.

(Above): F.J. Widgery – Cranmere Pool.
(Top right): John White Abbot – The Quay, Exeter, 1803.
(Right): William Widgery – View in Gidley Park, 1868.

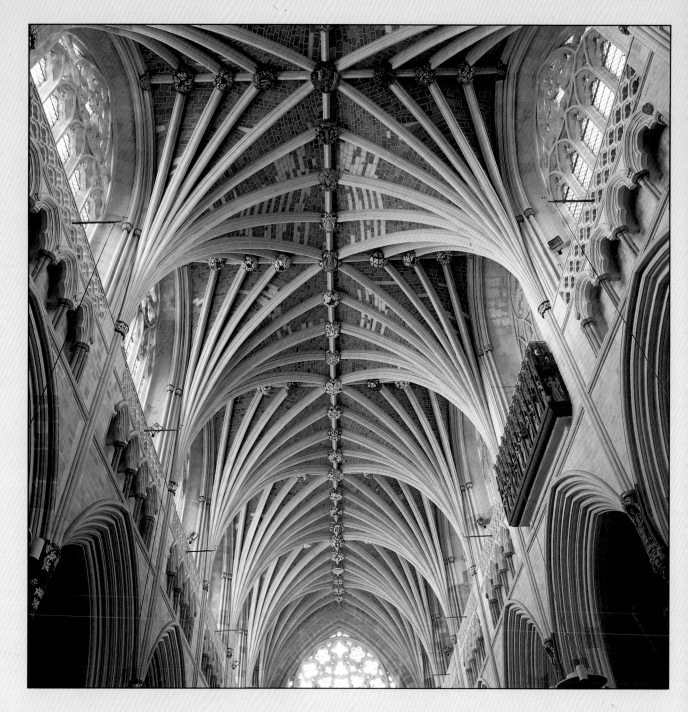

THE
CATHEDRAL

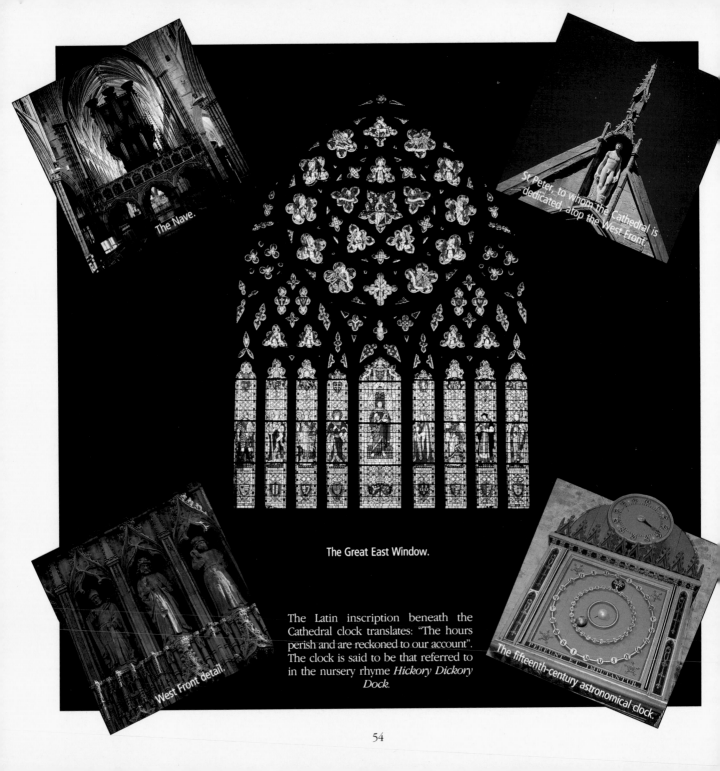

The Nave.

St Peter, to whom the Cathedral is dedicated, atop the West Front.

The Great East Window.

West Front detail.

The Latin inscription beneath the Cathedral clock translates: "The hours perish and are reckoned to our account". The clock is said to be that referred to in the nursery rhyme *Hickory Dickory Dock*.

The fifteenth-century astronomical clock.

This aerial view shows the area encompassed by the Close, originally walled off from the city.

T he Saxons were the first to build a church on the site and traces of this have been excavated outside the West Front. The Norman legacy remains in the two great towers of the present Cathedral, completed shortly after 1200. The work of transformation from Norman to Gothic began at the end of the thirteenth century and continued through the fourteenth century.

Bishop John de Grandisson kept Pope John XXII informed of progress: *"the cathedral of Exeter, now finished up to the nave, is marvellous in its beauty and when completed will surpass every church of its kind in England and France"*. The finished Cathedral has remained largely unchanged from that day to this.

A view of the West Front.

The CHURCHES OF EXETER

Memorial, St Martins.

I n medieval times Exeter boasted 32 parish churches and today the large number of Christian churches are supplemented by other places of worship from a variety of beliefs and cultures.

Devon as a whole became one of the most firmly Protestant counties in England and, in Georges Meeting, Exeter boasts one of the finest non-conformist chapels in the country. The parish churches in the city are fascinating in their variety of age and historical background and a number of Victorian churches are among the finest of their type.

St Leonard's floodlit.

St Petrock's High Street.

Synagogue.

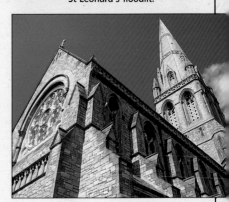

St Michael and All Angels.

St Sidwell c.1830.

Methodist Church, Sidwell Street.

Heavitree Church, 1851.

St Stephen's Bow.

St Thomas Church.

EXETER'S GHOSTS
AND
GHASTLY EVENTS

I n her book *Devon Ghosts* Theo Brown recalls that Exeter plays a part in that most famous of horror stories, *Dracula*. The respectable solicitor who in the story goes off to Transylvania, represents a practice in the Cathedral Close.

It is the Close that is the scene of Exeter's most sensational murder sparked by a disagreement between the Bishop and the Dean. On 10 November 1283. Walter de Lechlade, Precentor of the Cathedral, was cut down by a group of ruffians who entered the City under cover of darkness at the South Gate. A trial followed and five men were hanged including the mayor and the porter of the South Gate.

The Close itself is said to be haunted by a cowled monk – a Monastery was established here c.927. Another monk is said to haunt the Cowick Barton, a public house on the city outskirts.

Circumstances surrounding the death of William Petre of Whipton House add to Exeter's ghastly annals. On a January night in 1611 Petre had been drinking at the Dolphin Inn with his friends, Sir Edward Seymour of Berry Pomeroy and John and Edward Drewe of Killerton. After much carousing, and stopping at several other hostelries, the party rode out of the East Gate up the dark St Sidwell highway. Dawn found Will Petre lying dead with a ghastly wound

Devon and Exeter Institution.

A popular 'ghostly' tour ends with a certificate of survival.

to his head. The Drewes denied any knowledge of the death and it remains one of the city's unsolved mysteries.

A spectre haunts the site of Taddyforde house near Red Cow and St David's station. This is supposed to be the ghost of a certain Mr Kingdon who, in the last century, was said to dabble in magic.

A more benign spirit, that of a little old woman in black, haunts the Devon and Exeter Institution in Cathedral Close. Those familiar with the splendid olde worlde atmosphere of what was once a Regency club and library will have no difficulty in imagining this little figure.

Exeter Prison has housed a great number of criminals but none more famous than John 'Babbacombe' Lee who was tried for the murder of the elderly Miss Keyse at her seaside villa near Torquay in 1884. Lee pleaded not guilty but was tried and sentenced to be hanged at Exeter Gaol. Those awaiting the moment outside the prison were said to see a flock of doves fluttering over the site of execution at the moment Lee was to be hanged. In fact the trap, built to drop him to his death, failed to open on three separate occasions, and Lee was eventually reprieved. John Lee went on to live in notoriety as 'The Man They Could Not Hang'.

At the end of the Prayer Book Rebellion of 1549, Welsh, vicar of St Thomas, near the Exe Bridge, was sentenced to be hanged for his part in encouraging the rebels. His executioner, Bernard Duffield, erected a gallows on top of the vicar's own church tower and there hanged the unfortunate Welsh bedecked in 'popish apparel'.

A strange story forever connected with Topsham is the case of 'The Devil's Footprints' – a trail of cloven hoofprints defying natural explanation caused a flurry of national excitement and speculation.

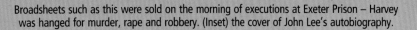

Broadsheets such as this were sold on the morning of executions at Exeter Prison – Harvey was hanged for murder, rape and robbery. (Inset) the cover of John Lee's autobiography.

An extract from *Gentleman's Magazine* (1737) Exeter. *Some fishermen near this city drawing their net ashore a creature of human shape, having two legs, leapt out and ran away very quickly; not being able to overtake it, they knocked it down by throwing sticks after it. At their coming up to it, it was dying, and groaned like a human creature; its feet were webbed like a duck's, it had eyes, nose and mouth, resembling those of a man, only the nose somewhat depressed; a tail not unlike that of a salmon's, turning up towards its back, and four feet high. It was publicly shown here.*

The EXETER BLITZ

Cathedral Close c.1943.
(Above – top left): A Fire Guard Team, Exeter 1943.
by William L. Clause.
(Above: Top Right):
Fore Street, 1942.

B efore the bombing of the Second World War 'Exeter was one of the most delightful and appealing cities in England, full of colour, light, and movement' – so wrote W.G. Hoskins, Devon's eminent historian. One can now only imagine the narrow lanes and streets of ancient houses, barely changed for centuries until the devastating night of 3/4 May 1942.

On the night of a full moon forty planes dropped 75 tonnes of bombs, 160 high explosive and 10 000 incendiary and parachute mines. Over 560 people were injured and 156 killed during the 74-minute raid.

Pilots of 504 (County of Nottingham) Squadron at Exeter airfield.

The raid was declared by Germany to be in retaliation for an RAF raid on Lubeck. Hitler had ordered that the most beautiful cities in England be targetted – the day after the raid German radio announced 'We have chosen as targets the most beautiful cities in England. Exeter was a jewel. We have destroyed it'.

Over 1500 houses were totally destroyed and 2700 seriously damaged, along with 9 churches, 6 banks, 26 public houses, 400 shops and many other business premises.

The Cathedral suffered some damage and the newly built city library was engulfed in flames. The exceptional group of Georgian buildings in Bedford Circus also suffered severe damage and were later demolished.

The day after the raid was 'a perfect spring day'. It took five hours to bring the fires under control and while citizens came to terms with the devastation, the services began clearing up: dealing with unexploded bombs and burying the dead.

The raid of the 3/4 May was one of nineteen raids suffered by Exeter. During the course of the war, bombing destroyed 30 acres of the inner city – three-quarters of the principal shopping area – and 265 people were killed, with over a thousand injured.

FIGURE 13.—GERMAN INCENDIARY BOMB WITH SEPARATING EXPLOSIVE NOSE (I.B.S.E.N.)

(Left) Blitzed areas of the city centre.
(Above) Details of incendiary bombs.
(Right) wartime cartoon.
(Below) A Heinkel 111.

'But apart from this, life is going on just the same as usual'

(Top) Looking west across High Street, 1945.

(Above) A view southwards across High Street, 1945.

(Left) Catherine Street, 1942.

THE
CHANGING
CITY

The
POST-WAR
RECONSTRUCTION

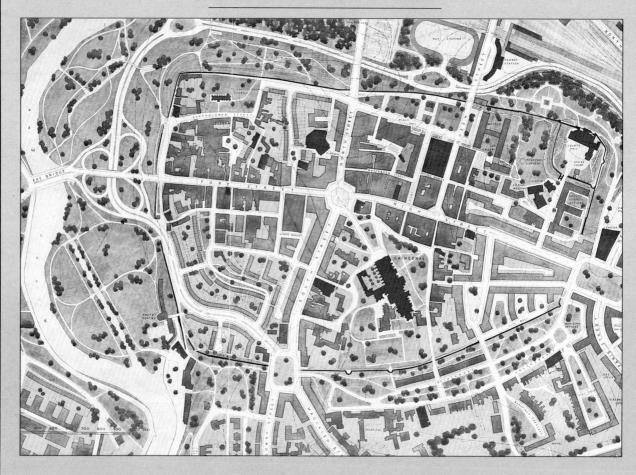

High Street, c. 1955.

Bedford Circus, pre-war.

Princesshay, looking north.

Princesshay, looking south.

A t the end of the war the City Council immediately began to plan the rebuilding of the city. To this end they engaged the services of a leading town planner, Thomas Sharp, to prepare proposals for reconstruction. Not all Sharp's suggestions were adopted but his plan (left) formed the basis of the redevelopment of the war-torn city.

Sharp's plan, 1949, clearly shows his proposal for a 'green moat' to be created around the city wall.

The High Street was the first area to be redeveloped after the war, with the top of Fore Street and Sidwell Street following. The South Street area had suffered heavy bomb damage and was almost completely levelled.

Perhaps Sharp's most significant contribution is Princesshay, one of the first pedestrian shopping streets in the country. It was named after Princess Elizabeth (now H.M. The Queen) who opened it on 21 October 1949 (above, right).

Sharp paid attention to the type of architecture he envisaged in the 'new' city. He suggested that the buildings "which will best stand the test of time will be those which show no stylistic tricks at all but which depend for the effect on being clean, well proportioned and honest".

Critics did not agree. Writing in 1960 Professor Hoskins said "much has been rebuilt in a commonplace style that might belong anywhere".

M istakes *were* made but great care has been taken more recently to ensure that new building is in sympathy with its surroundings, while the best of the old is retained and preserved.

Left top and middle: Castle Street (before and after).

Left: Tudor Street and Bartholomew Terrace.
Above top and bottom: The ABC cinema makes way for Dillons bookshop.

To deal with the increasing traffic congestion, Sharp had proposed a new by-pass around the edge of the city centre. Only the eastern section of this, Western Way, was constructed.

Land and buildings were bought in anticipation of other parts of the route, blighting buildings and creating many derelict sites in and around the city.

Following the abandonment of the proposed new roads many of the vacant sites have been used to create areas of new building. Sympathetically designed and landscaped, these sites provide much needed housing, particularly for the elderly.

1970's, before pedestrianisation.

Blighted buildings, Magdalen Street.

Exe Street from Bartholomew Terrace.

Above and right: Exe Street (before and after).

CONSERVATION

Tudor House, before…

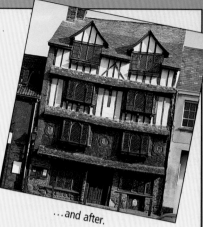

…and after.

M any old buildings in the city have benefited from a concerted programme of conservation. By preserving their historic and architectural interest, these buildings contribute to the atmosphere of the city.

St Thomas Station (before and after).

Higher Market interior (before and after).

Higher Market, Queen Street (before and after).

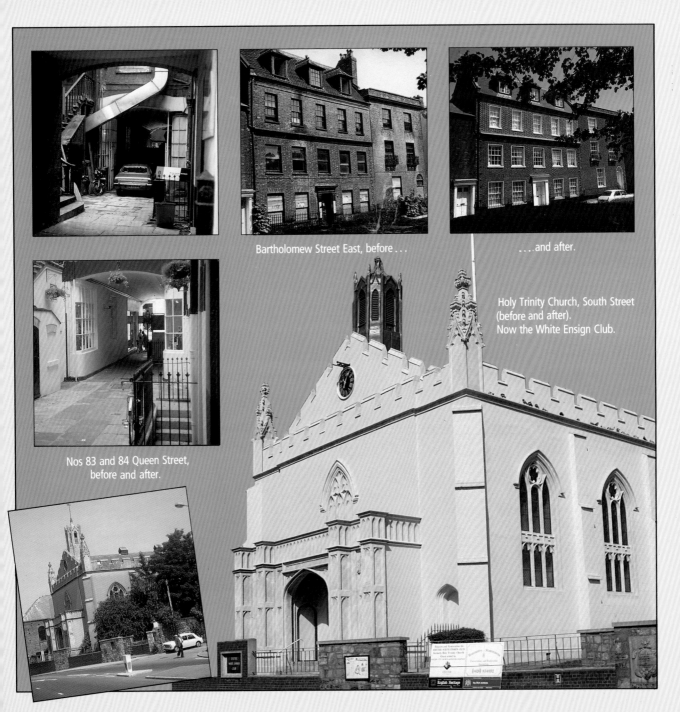

Bartholomew Street East, before . . .

. . . and after.

Holy Trinity Church, South Street (before and after). Now the White Ensign Club.

Nos 83 and 84 Queen Street, before and after.

Along with the preservation of individual buildings, many historic areas of the city have been enhanced through attractive landscape works.

City Wall, Southernhay.

Medieval Bridge (before and after).

Dereliction adjoining St Nicholas' Priory has been replaced by a garden.

Top: Quayside.
Middle: City Wall, Southernhay West.

ENHANCEMENT

A s Thomas Sharp realised, a prime requirement for the future was the separation of pedestrians and motorcars so that people might walk and shop in a safe and attractive environment. This strategy has been realised in many city centres and Exeter has greatly benefited from its own pedestrianisation programme.

Gandy Street, before . . .

. . . and after.

Resurfacing, Cathedral Close:

High St before (right) and after (above).

St Edmunds-on-the-Bridge.

Catherines Almshouses

The Cathedral

St Michaels

New light on old buildings – Floodlighting schemes in the city help to transform the night skyline

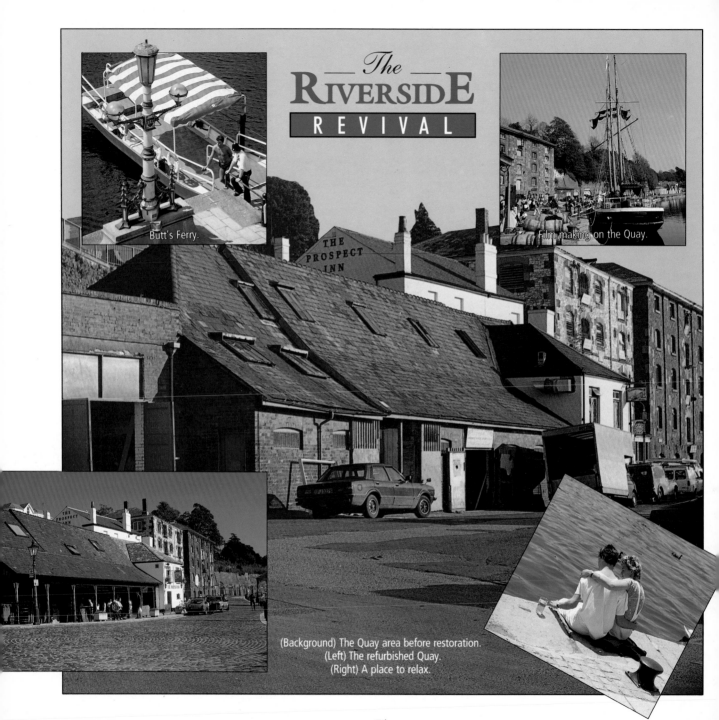

The RIVERSIDE REVIVAL

Butt's Ferry.

Film making on the Quay.

THE PROSPECT INN

(Background) The Quay area before restoration.
(Left) The refurbished Quay.
(Right) A place to relax.

(Above) Cricklepit foot and cycle bridge.

The Riverside has undergone a transformation in recent years. By the early 1970s the old riverside industries had moved out and most of the land surrounding the new river bridges and the flood prevention scheme was derelict, providing an opportunity for imaginative rejuvenation.

The warehouses on the quay, one built of red sandstone the other of white limestone, are also part of the recent transformation of the area. These massive five-storey buildings were constructed c.1835 by two Exeter builders the Hoopers and the Cornishes. Converted to offices with shops, a public house and restaurant on the ground floor, the buildings retain many of the features associated with their former trade.

(Top left) Quayside and Custom House.
(Top) Sculpture at the Custom House.
(Above) 'On The Waterfront'.
(Right) The Wharfinger's Office, home of the Canal and Quay Trust.

HAVEN BANKS

The old malthouse, Haven Banks.
(Inset) Architect's model of the Haven Banks development.

C ricklepit Bridge, opened in 1989, links the historic quayside to Haven Banks. The imaginative development of Haven Banks provides riverside housing, shops, restaurants and a new paved pedestrian piazza at the head of the Canal basin. A pedestrian walkway through the award-winning housing development leads to the Canal Basin where cargoes were loaded and unloaded. The old warehouses were, until 1991, home to the Exeter Maritime Museum.

Industries once flourished alongside the canal and railway. A gasworks was established in 1836 and an electrical power station in 1905.

A remnant of the South Devon Railway, the City Basin Branch of 1867, survives.

The old malthouse sits on the Haven Banks beyond Shooting Marsh Stile. It has an interesting if obscure history – first appearing as 'The New Brewery' on a map of 1792. By 1890 the building was being used as a malthouse and it remained as such until the 1950s.

A swan nesting close to Cricklepit Bridge (right). Even in the heart of the city, wildlife abounds.

Left: Cricklepit Bridge leading to Haven Banks.
Above Riverside housing.
Below top: Waterwheel.
Below bottom: Cricklepit Mill.
Below right: The Dry House.

CRICKLEPIT MILL

Cricklepit Mill has a fascinating history (the first mill was built here as early as 1190) and has always been a grist mill. It was one of two city mills licenced for grinding wheat, taking its water from an ancient leat. Its machinery remains largely intact, including an undershot waterwheel of 4 metres diameter. Restoration means this important site will remain as part of Exeter's living history.

Close by is a long eighteenth-century building, a 'dry-house' where cloth from the fulling mills could be dried under cover, stretched tight on beams from 'tenter-hooks'. This is the only building of its type to survive in the West Country.

HOUSE AND HOME

E xeter can claim as wide a variety of housing types as any City in the country. Add to this the delightful 'rural' feel given by the views out to the surrounding countryside and you have the ideal place to live. Traditional town house residences remain in the suburbs where the Georgian and Victorian middle classes lived.

Early twentieth century housing in pleasant suburbs lie close to the city centre, whilst new housing is available on residential developments on the city outskirts.

New developments on inner-city sites provide accommodation to suit the confirmed urban dweller.

(Above l to r): Sylvania; Wrefords Close; Earl Richards Road North (designed by Louis de Soisson who created Welwyn Garden City). (Left) Regency villa in St Leonards.

Sandford Walk, Newtown.

Kinnerton Way, Exwick.

Shilhay.

Napier Terrace and Exe Street.

Beedles Terrace.

Exe Street.

Flowerpot.

Brooke Avenue

Collins Road, Sylvania.

Shoppers in High Street.

LIFESTYLE

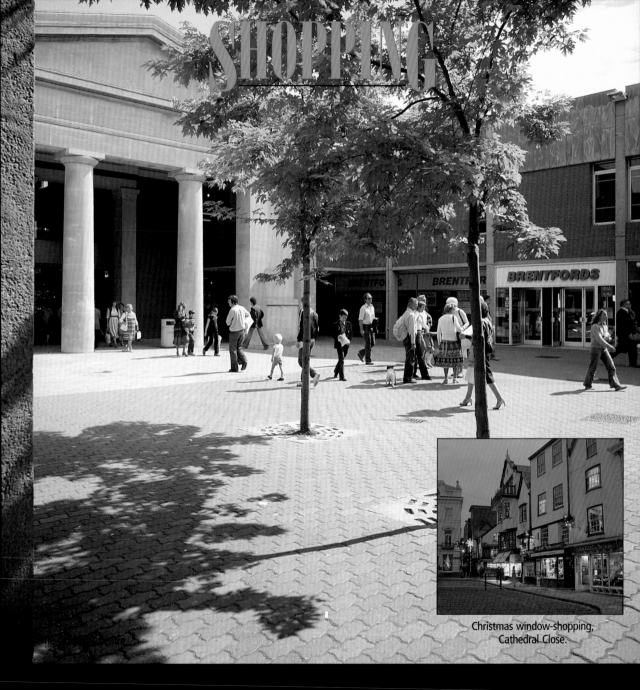

SHOPPING

BRENTFORDS

Christmas window-shopping,
Cathedral Close.

High Street.

High Street.

Body Shop, Higher Market.

Harlequins.

I n recent years great efforts have been made to enhance the shopping areas of the city centre. Well-planned pedestrianised streets have created an environment that has attracted the most prestigious high street names to the city, providing shoppers with a wide range of choice within pleasant surroundings.

The Marks and Spencer development, though criticised by many architects, was warmly accepted by the residents.

Gandy Street.

Chandni Chowk, Paul Street.

Laura Ashley, High Street.

Marks & Spencer, High Street.

EATING
AND
DRINKING

Exe salmon

D evon is blessed with an abundance of good food and, although the cliché of Cider and Cream continues to be part of the tourist appeal, the excellence of Devon's produce means no end of good things to eat. Closeness to the sea (and of course the renowned Exe salmon) provides plentiful fish and shellfish, whilst as a centre for market gardening, there is no shortage of fresh vegetables and fruit. Superb Devon beef and lamb provide the ready ingredients for traditional recipes, but there are wide choices across a range of continental and Eastern restaurants throughout the city, and excellent hotels.

Fine Food

Food, Italian style, Topsham

Ship Inn, Martin's Lane

A riverside pub

DAVY'S OLD
WALLOP
PINT MUG £1·00
½ gal JUG £3·80

CLIENTS ARE
Respectfully Requested
TO REFRAIN
FROM SPITTING

DAVY'S ST JULIEN
£8·25

MÂCON VILLAGES
£6·75

Ch Haut Piquant
£8·45

Bottlescreu Bills; (Inset) The White Hart

Guildhall ceramic mural
(Phillipe Threlfall)

ART ON DISPLAY

Sports sculpture (Roger Dean).

A High Street Pavement Artist.

Fore Street mural (Andrew Stacey).

Ballerina (Marie Noelle Davies).

Guildhall car park (Elaine Goodwin).

Tin Lane (Elaine Goodwin).

High Street (Richards and Faulkner)

Marilyn – St Thomas.

M ulti-storey car parks are not usually thought to be places where works of art are found but visitors to the Guildhall car park find their shopping trips enhanced by a 20 metre mosaic mural by Elaine Goodwin. The mural depicts a walk along the High Street, down Fore Street to St Thomas.

Murals can be found in other city car parks while two magnificent murals decorate the ends of buildings in Fore Street and Holloway Street – these by Andrew Stacey.

More impromptu art is to be discovered among the pavement artists and buskers in the city – each helping to create an atmosphere of fun and pleasure.

Traditional statues are so familiar their artistic qualities sometimes go unnoticed, while modern sculptures often demand attention. Exeter provides many examples of both.

Lower Coombe Street (Andrew Alleway).

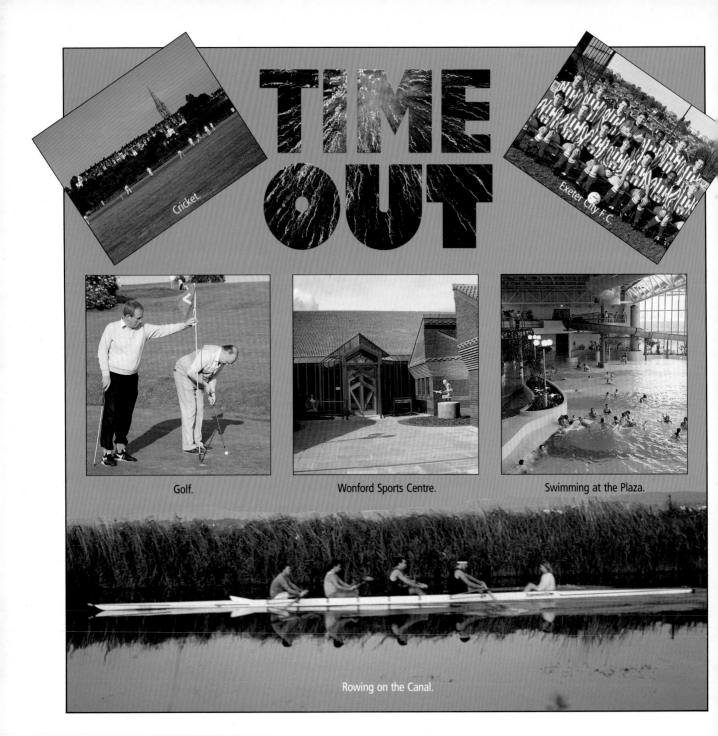

TIME OUT

Cricket.

Exeter City F.C.

Golf.

Wonford Sports Centre.

Swimming at the Plaza.

Rowing on the Canal.

Living in Exeter gives every opportunity to indulge a preference for active or sedentary pursuits. Sports fields provide opportunities for cricket, football and other outdoor games, whilst a number of leisure centres give swimmers and fitness enthusiasts a wide range of choice. On the cultural side, the Northcott Theatre has a national reputation and other theatres and auditoria provide excellent venues for plays, music and other forms of entertainment.

Northcott Theatre.

Exeter Arts Centre.

A wide choice of live musical events is available.

GARDEN PRIDE
THE CITY PARKS

T he early horticulturalists recognised that Exeter's soil and climate combined to provide a most fertile nursery for plants of all kinds. The famous Veitch family had various nurseries in and around the city and many market gardens thrive today.

Rougemont Gardens
Rougemont takes its name from the red colour of the volcanic stone outcrop which forms the hill. The Normans built the castle here and Athelstan's tower was added later. Part of the castle ditch serves as a feature of the garden. Among a wide range of exotic trees are the Judas, Strawberry, Maidenhair and Medlar trees.

Rougemont Gardens (above and left). Northernhay Gardens (inset).

Southernhay

Southernhay (left) is flanked by well-proportioned Georgian terraces and many prosperous families lived here in former years. There are over fifty trees in the central gardens, comprising thirty different species – including Exeter Oaks.

The Lucombe, or Exeter Oak, is a subspecies of the evergreen oak, known for its fast-growing properties. Mr. Lucombe, an Exeter nurseryman, grew the original tree and had it cut down and sawn into planks for his coffin. Fine specimens of the oak can be seen at Killerton.

Pinces Garden (inset above) is named after another Exeter plantsman, Robert Taylor Pince, who joined Lucombe in a nursery in the 1820s. They introduced the first English tea rose in 1841. A beautiful wisteria archway is a feature of this garden.

Northernhay Gardens (left) have been a public pleasure garden since 1612 and contains a wide variety of trees and shrubs, many of them labelled.

Other gardens and open spaces around the city provide interest for the horti-culturalist and havens of tranquility for the weary shopper. These include the 'secret' gardens alongside the city wall in Southernhay and St Nicholas Priory, adjacent to Rougemont House, and the North Street 'pocket' park (inset middle).

Most popular of the open spaces is the Cathedral Close (inset below), but Friernhay Green and St Bartholomews are also within a short walk of the city centre.

The word 'Hay' in so many Exeter placenames comes from the Saxon 'ge-haeg' – an enclosure beyond the city wall.

The
UNIVERSITY GARDENS

The University Gardens
The sweeping lawns and gardens of
Exeter University are an horticulturist's
delight. Here thrive many species not
found elsewhere in Britain.

The VALLEY PARKS

The Valley Parks are a deliberate attempt to bring green wedges of countryside into the heart of the city. The parks, Duryard, Ludwell, Mincinglake, the Riverside and Alphington/Whitestone, are within easy reach of the suburbs and are laid out with scenic walks.

It is difficult to imagine that Mincinglake was once the city refuse tip but landscaping and tree planting in the 1980s have completely changed the area. In 1990 hundreds of cubic metres of wet habitat were moved block by block from the new housing development at Exwick to the Mincinglake Valley. The area supports a wide range of plants including broad-leafed sedge, marsh orchids and birds foot trefoil. This in turn is frequented by insects and butterflies including marbled whites, common blues and small coppers.

Duryard's twin valleys, lying a mile to the north of the city, contain a mixture of woodland, meadows and ancient hedgerows supporting a wide variety of wildlife, including roe deer. The valley is a remnant of an estate belonging to the city in the Middle Ages. Its name reflects its ancient use as a deer park. It is possible to walk through this area from the immediate edge of the city into open countryside.

Ludwell's rolling meadows form an island of countryside protected by gentle hills. From walks along the ridge there are fine views across the city and towards the Exe estuary.

Alphington/Whitestone Valley Park forms a delightful rural fringe to the western side of the city.

A wide variety of activities can be enjoyed in the Riverside Valley Park, sailing, canoeing and angling, as well as birdwatching and walking. In addition to the footpath network there is also a cycle route. Much has been done to improve cycle routes around the city in order to encourage this healthy and popular activity.

Ludwell Valley Park.

Mincinglake Valley Park.

Bell Vue Road, Duryard.

Picnic site, Duryard.

Riverside Valley Park.

Riverside

EXETER
—IN—
BLOOM

S ince winning international acclaim as European Floral City, Exeter has set itself a high standard to follow. The City reflects the same pride in its daily appearance with streets bedecked with floral displays from June to September.

Sculpture, Guildhall Centre

City gardener, Southernhay

Princesshay

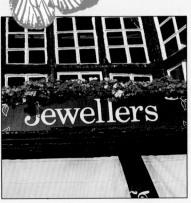

Windowbox, Cathedral Close

Floral display, High Street

G E T T I N G
AROUND

A growing awareness of the need to curb the use of private cars has resulted in the adoption of a number of schemes intended to enhance the quality of the city environment. The best use is made of available space for car parking, while Park and Ride presents a real alternative to congestion. Cycle routes can also make a significant contribution towards easing traffic problems whilst adding pleasure to leisure cycling. An innovative Green Bike scheme allows bikes to be 'borrowed' for use in the city.

GREEN BIKE SCHEME

COMMUNITY CYCLE

POINT 2

(Clockwise from top right) Mini-buses in High Street; Park and Ride; Cycle route; (inset) Green Bike scheme; Traffic jam; Permits allow resident-only parking.

WELCOME TO
EXETER

(Above) Interpret Britain awards.
(Below) Redcoat guides are on hand to take
the visitor on 'themed' tours of the city.

T ourism is an important part of the economy of the West Country as a whole and Exeter is a centre of attraction for thousands of visitors.

With so many sites of historic interest, and being close to the scenic attractions of the coast and moor, Exeter has a natural advantage as a tourist centre. The Cathedral provides a focal point for all visitors but care has been taken to provide a wide spectrum of attractions to suit all tastes.

Central to the City's efforts to provide the visitor with a memorable stay is the guided tours which provide a range of conducted tours throughout the city on a number of themes including Victorian Exeter, The Blitz, and Exeter Ghosts and Legends.

For those exploring independently, the comprehensive signposting around the city guides the visitor to the important sites.

Distinctive panels strategically placed around the city also provide 'at a glimpse' information about the city and its history. Exeter has received a National Award for the Interpretation of Britain's Heritage.

Elegant signposts help visitors find their way around the City.

Information panels provide background information on the City's attractions.

Rennes

EXETER
IN
EUROPE

Terracina

K een to further international co-
operation, Exeter has developed close commercial and
cultural links with four European Cities.

Rennes
Twinned with Exeter since 1956, Rennes
(population 200,000) is the Capital of
Brittany. The city has many fine buildings including the Palais de Justice and
the Cathedral, built between 1540 and
1700. The City is the major cultural and
commercial centre of Brittany, boasting
the largest Citroen factory in France
and the annual "Tombees de la Nuit"
(Nighfalls) Festival.

Many local organisations, including
Exeter University, have developed links
with their counterparts in Rennes.

Bad Homburg
Officially twinned since 1965, Bad
Homburg's links with England stretch
back to the Victorian era, when it was a
fashionable spa and resort for well-to-
do English visitors. Still a renowned
spa, the city, which nestles amongst the
hills of the Taunus Region, has superb
parks, shopping precincts and leisure
facilities.

In 1990 the entire Bad Homburg
Choir visited Exeter to stage a joint-

Bad
Homburg

Yaroslavl

BAD HOMBURG WAY

Unveiled by Herr Wolfgang Assmus
Oberbürgermeister of Bad Homburg
30th September 1987

performance of Haydn's *Creation* with
the Exeter Music Group.

Bad Homburg is within easy reach of
Frankfurt International Airport.

Terracina
Twinned with Exeter since 1988, Terra-
cina is an historic town 60 miles south
of Rome, famed also for its long sandy
beaches and wide promenades. In
Roman times Terracina, where the Via
Appia met the coast, was the gateway to
Southern Italy and high above the city
are the remains of the Temple of Jove.
The city makes an excellent touring
base for Rome, Naples, Pompeii and
Capri.

Yaroslavl
260kms North-East of Moscow, on
the Volga River, Yaroslavl (population
626,000) is one of Russia's most important cultural and historic cities, forming
part of the famous "Golden Ring", a
region famed for its art and architecture.

The Exeter Children's Orchestra have
performed in Yaroslavl, and runners
from the Kolobok Athletics Club in
Yaroslavl have competed in the Great
West Run at the invitation of the Exeter
Harriers, two members of which have
married Russians as a direct result of
these exchanges.

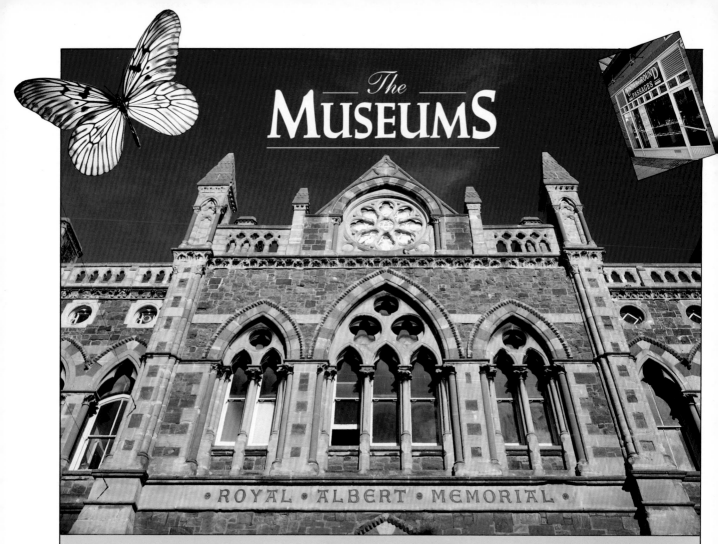

The MUSEUMS

·ROYAL·ALBERT·MEMORIAL·

W ith its rich history it is hardly a surprise that Exeter has an abundance of good museums. These include a number of individual sites of historical interest open to the public.

The principal city museum is **The Royal Albert Memorial Museum** in Queen Street. This Victorian treasure house includes natural history, both local and exotic, including a giraffe; outstanding archaeology on the Romans, and ethnography from North American Indians and Eskimos, to the Pacific islands and Africa. Beautiful Exeter silver and westcountry pottery compliment fine art, including topological prints and drawings of Exeter scenes. Here the visitor can see some of the traditional museum exhibits – a fine natural history collection – along with specialist collections.

Emphasis is placed on the importance of the Museum as a major regional resource both for educational visits and for the general visitor.

The art collection contains a number of significant paintings by artists such as Joshua Reynolds.

The **Rougemont House Museum** was reopened in 1987 in an elegant Georgian House set in beautiful gardens below the Norman castle gatehouse.

The costume and lace collection is one of the best outside London, while the Honiton lace collection is the largest in the world.

Its future uncertain, Exeter's *Maritime Museum* attracted thousands of visitors each year to view the hundred or so working boats on display from all parts of the world, from Arab dhows to reed boats and dug-outs. Many exhibits are afloat on the Canal Basin.

Nearby is the **Quay House Interpretation Centre,** where exciting displays provide a picture of the City's past linked to the quay area.

The important role played by Topsham in Exeter's past makes **Topsham Museum** well worth a visit. The collection, featuring maritime interests, is housed in a delightful 'Dutch' house in the Strand and is furnished as a merchant's home at the time of the port's greatest prosperity.

For those with a martial interest the **Devonshire and Dorset Regiment Museum** at the Wyvern Barracks displays the history of that fine regiment's proudest and illustrious feats.

Also open for the public are the following sites, buildings and collections of specialist interest: **Exeter Cathedral** and the **Cathedral Library, The Guildhall, Tuckers Hall, St Nicholas Priory** and the **Underground Passages.**

(Left) Rougemont House Museum.

(Above) Cloth bales at the Quay House.
(Below) Artefacts from the Royal Albert Memorial Museum.

Wontford Hospital, c.1860.

The CARING CITY

Royal Devon and Exeter Hospital.

Since Dean Alured Clarke established one of the first provincial hospitals in 1741, Exeter has been at the forefront of public health care. The West of England Eye Infirmary was established in 1808.

Today Exeter enjoys an excellent reputation for its health care services. Modern facilities are supported by highly trained staff across a range of professional skills while links with the University bring significant benefits in the field of medical research.

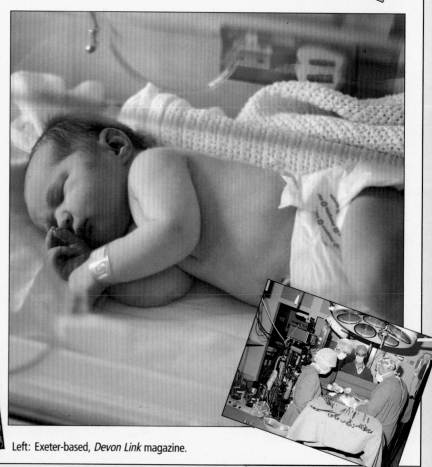

DEVON LINK
SUMMER
I'VE STARTED, SO I'LL FINISH...
Page 4
ADVENTURES IN KESWICK
Page 18
DOWN ON THE FARM
Page 36
A quarterly magazine for disabled people

Left: Exeter-based, *Devon Link* magazine.

LEARNING
— TO LIVE IN —
EXETER

St Thomas High School

Exeter College

E xeter played a foremost role in the struggle for freedom of education. In the seventeenth century the City Chamber fought hard against ecclesiastical opposition for the establishment of Free Schools. In 1631 a Grammar School and a Blue School (so called from the uniform worn by its scholars) were founded on the site of the Hospital of St John near East Gate. The Blue Boy statue in Princesshay (inset below right) is a reminder of early schooling in the city.

Today the city enjoys a wide range of educational opportunities for children from pre-school age through to tertiary colleges and, of course, the University. There are more than a dozen private schools in the city. All State schools in Exeter are comprehensive, with sixth-form facilities provided by Exeter College which has 2500 full time students with twice that number attending part time.

The Faculty of Arts and Design, Polytechnic South West, provides degree and diploma courses in the arts, design and humanities with educational links with other establishments at regional, national and international level.

Students at the Cathedral School

Bluecoat statue

Fireworks over the City.

EVENTS
— AND —
FESTIVALS

Punch and Judy, Exeter Festival

The Exeter Festival is held annually in mid June and has firmly established itself as one of the country's top events of its kind, enjoyed by local people and visitors alike.

A wide-ranging programme of events includes concerts by major orchestras and international artists from the world of theatre, sport, music and dance. It is a chance for the city to open its doors to an exciting world of culture and fun – an event enjoyed by all.

Sheriff's Coach.

(Above) The Dragon Boat Race. (Above left) The Cathedral is a focus for many religious festivals. (Left) Entertaining children in the Harlequin Centre. (Below left) The Great West Run. (Below) Lammas Fair.

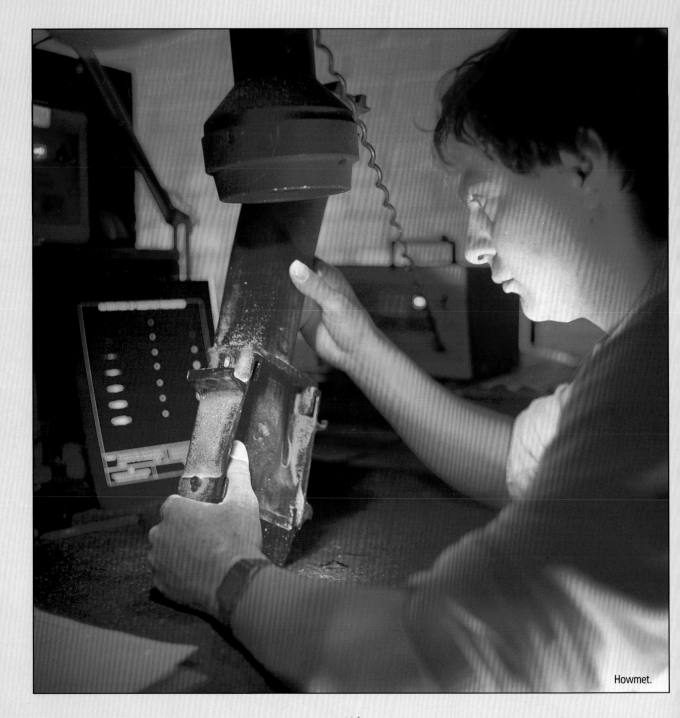

Howmet.

THE WORKING CITY

BUSINESS AS USUAL

T he continuity of traditional business and industrial activity plays an essential part in establishing a healthy and pleasant 'place of work'. New business is attracted as much by the atmosphere of a city, as by the pragmatic demands of location, ease of access and the availability of a skilled workforce. In all this, Exeter is a fortunate city.

Among the principal industrial activities of the past a constant supply of water has been a striking common factor: milling, fulling of cloth, brewing, cotton spinning, papermaking and tanning. Most of the basic manufacturing industries have now gone, but they leave behind many associated businesses of an astonishing variety, exhibiting a wide range of specialist skills.

A thurible in polished brass.

Amongst the oldest companies in Exeter is Wippells, a business founded on the rich woollen trade of Exeter and now continuing as a manufacturer of ecclesiastical and ceremonial garments and furnishings supplied thoughout the world. Skills developed over two hundred years go into creating superb embroideries, silverwork and stained glass.

A magnificent rose window created by Wippells for an episcopal church in Nashville, Tennessee.

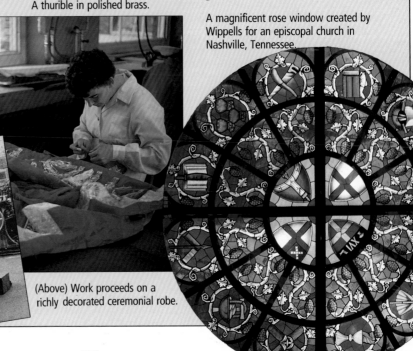

(Above) Work proceeds on a richly decorated ceremonial robe.

Printing c.1920.

108

Printing and publishing are important traditional industries within the City, linked originally with paper manufacturers. A current trade directory lists over forty printing companies operating in the city.

BPCC Wheatons Ltd (left) is one of the largest of Exeter's many printing companies. Originally A. Wheaton & Co. the business was founded in the 1830s and operated until the 1960s from its Fore Street premises. Now a major arm of a national printing company, Wheatons offers a complete range of printing skills from typesetting to binding.

Specialist services allied to the printing trade also form part of the city's important business community. At Peninsular Repro (below left) highly skilled colour-scanning operations are provided.

Devon Books, a joint publishing venture between private enterprise and the County Council has a base in Exeter from which many books of local interest are published.

Topics Visual Information, a creative communications specialist, is also based in Exeter offering a broad spectrum of services in graphic design, video and television production.

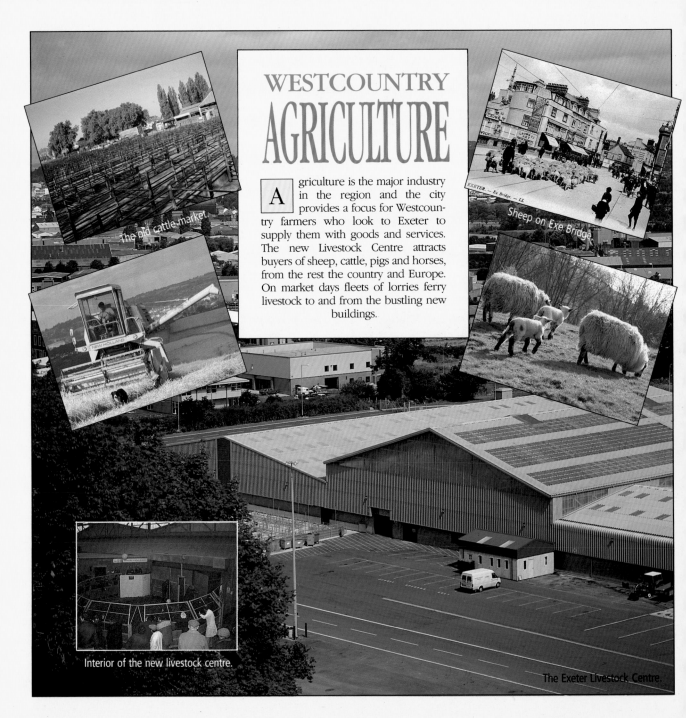

WESTCOUNTRY
AGRICULTURE

A griculture is the major industry in the region and the city provides a focus for Westcountry farmers who look to Exeter to supply them with goods and services. The new Livestock Centre attracts buyers of sheep, cattle, pigs and horses, from the rest the country and Europe. On market days fleets of lorries ferry livestock to and from the bustling new buildings.

The old cattle market

Sheep on Exe Bridge

Interior of the new livestock centre.

The Exeter Livestock Centre.

110

THE DEVON
COUNTY
SHOW

Hurdle-making.

Traction engines on display.

T he agricultural origins of this three-day annual show are still evident in the many farming attractions, and principally in the showing and judging of livestock. Now it is also a showpiece for businesses of all types. In a bustling tented town every kind of enterprise from banks and computer firms to building companies and food producers is on display.

Until 1989 held at Whipton, over 100 000 people visit the new purpose built Westpoint showground to view the livestock shows, demonstrations of rural skills, show jumping, sideshows and trade exhibitions.

Spot the busker!

Crowds throng the main concourse.

The main showing – cattle on show.

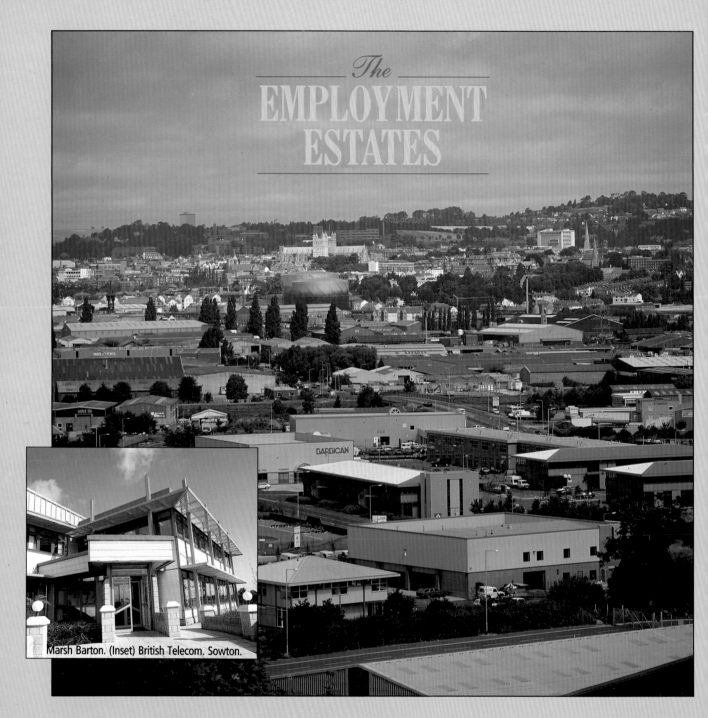

The
EMPLOYMENT
ESTATES

Marsh Barton. (Inset) British Telecom. Sowton.

In the decades following the war three industrial estates were established to the east and south of the city at Pinhoe, Sowton and Marsh Barton. More recently land has been set aside for both new and established businesses to expand at the 55-acre Matford Business Park.

Matford Business Park – The most recently developed site. Matford is home to the new Livestock Centre. Among the other businesses are the Transfleet distribution warehouse for Marks & Spencer (above), the SMB dealership for BMW cars, and the EBC Group. Many small companies have established themselves in the modern, attractive purpose-built developments on the site.

Marsh Barton – The oldest of the industrial estates, Marsh Barton was earmarked by Thomas Sharp in his plan for rebuilding the city after the war as 'the obvious locality' for a new industrial area. It is the home of many of Exeter's older established industrial companies including services to the motor industry. The Enterprise Workshop scheme has helped a number of small businesses to get started.

Sowton – Recent developments at Sowton have included a new regional office and laboratories for the National Rivers Authority, SWEB, the Express & Echo Newspaper, and a regional stores and computer centre for British Telecom. Expansion to Sowton is taking place on 45 acres of land north of the Honiton Road. Sowton is ideally placed alongside the M5.

Pynes Hill – A number of prestigious companies occupy premises at Pynes Hill including Medical Sickness and the National Farmer's Union regional headquarters.

Matford.

COMMERCIAL
BUSINESS
SERVICE SECTOR

S upporting Exeter's industrial base is a complex infrastructure of professional services including insurance companies, solicitors, estate agents, and accountants, most of them located close to the city centre. The percentage of those employed in the service sector in Exeter accounts for 85% of the workforce against 68% nationally.

Exeter has been particularly successful in attracting financial services companies. These in turn attract similar companies and stimulate growth in office support industries such as reprographics, staff agencies, publishing, marketing and advertising firms. A number of distribution companies have also relocated to Exeter.

The imposing terraces of Southernhay, the city's principal office location, reflect the prosperity of the Georgian period. Many commercial sector companies have their base here, an attractive workplace amid tree-lined gardens.

(Above and left) Southernhay Gardens.

Traditional Offices in Dix's Field.

New Offices in Dix's Field.

EXETER
PEOPLE
Making it work

P eople are the key ingredient in any business, large or small. Skill, enthusiasm and enjoyment of one's job, and pride in one's place of work, play an essential part in the success of the community as a whole.

Refuse collection – a vital task.

(Above) Habitat. Office workers at London and Manchester.

Health food store.

Market trader.

Chippy.

Fruit and veg.

Travel agent.

Sport and leisure.

Fish shop.

Police.

Postman.

CRIME
— AND —
JUSTICE

County Gaol c. 1830

Exeter Prison.

Crime and Justice – Exeter has been an administrative centre since Roman times. The Courts of Justice, the Assizes and the Quarter Sessions, and the Provost Court were at one time held in the Guildhall, apart from two occasions when, because of the plague in Exeter, they were held in Tiverton.

Throughout history the city has steadfastly guarded its exclusive right to administer local justice. Civil cases are heard at the County Court while major criminal cases are dealt with by the Crown Court, both at The Castle. The Magistrates Court, in Heavitree Road, deals with petty crimes or preliminary hearings.

Four chambers are based within the city with about forty barristers.

Legal Sunday (above right) is a ceremony of immense importance to the legal profession. Traditionally it takes place in the summer session of the courts. The judge, who resides at Larkbeare during this period, is joined for worship at the Cathedral by the Lord Lieutenant, the High Sheriff and members of the legal profession.

Exeter Prisons – The original city gaol was established at South Gate in the sixteenth century. In the eighteenth century it was described as 'dark, dirty and offensive … nothing could exceed the squalid wretchedness of the prisoners.' In 1819 a new city prison, the Borough Gaol was completed at St Thomas and this remained in use until 1863 when all prisoners were transferred to the County Gaol. This forbidding edifice, in New North Road, today houses remand prisoners and those serving sentences.

DEMARCATED ON THE PAVEMENT TO THE RIGHT OF THIS NOTICE IS THE FOUNDATION OF THE ROMAN GATE TOWER FLANKING THE SOUTH GATE TO THE CITY. THE GATE WAS REBUILT IN MEDIEVAL TIMES AND THEN USED AS A DEBTORS PRISON. IT WAS DEMOLISHED IN A.D. 1819.

FOCUS FOR THE REGION

A
FOCUS
FOR THE
REGION

I n law, commerce, education and culture, Exeter is a focus for the whole of Devon; but the city also serves a region well beyond its county boundaries, providing a national centre for administration, learning and industry. The following pages reflect the regional importance of the city – a status Exeter has held for almost two thousand years.

UNIVERSITY *of* EXETER

AND SPECIAL SCHOOLS

A mongst the top flight of British Universities, Exeter University campus occupies a magnificent 400-acre site on the hills overlooking the city from the north. The campus is notably compact. All the main buildings, together with the sports hall, and the student amenity buildings are within easy reach of each other. Here also is the nationally acclaimed Northcott Theatre.

Of the six faculties, five (Arts, Engineering, Law, Science and Social Studies), are situated on the main campus. The sixth, Education, is housed on the site of the former St Luke's College.

Recently there has been the establishment of a number of interdisciplinary research centres, including the Centre for Management Studies, the Complementary Health Centre, Earth Resources Centre and the Police and Criminal Justice Studies Centre. There is also a Postgraduate Medical School where staff are actively engaged in a wide range of research activities directly related to the medical care of local people.

(Top left) An aerial view of the University campus.
(Top right) A dye laser in the Dept of Physics.
(Right) The University campus at night.

Students enjoying a break from studies.

Exeter is also fortunate to be the home of a number of nationally important educational establishments catering for those with special needs. Modern facilities and technology, combined with the skills and care of trained staff, allow children to live and grow into respected and participating members of society.

The West of England School for children with little or no sight – began life in 1839 as a class for teaching the blind children of the city. From these humble beginnings the school now occupies a 14-acre site with 150 blind or partially sighted pupils, aged from 3–19 years, many with additional handicaps. Ten local authorities, mainly from the South West region, sponsor pupils.

The school offers a full National Curriculum to GCSE standard. At sixteen students are integrated with tutorial support into local colleges.

The school is very well equipped with the latest technology. Computers are linked to speech synthesizers, printers, braille embossers and closed circuit television.

A Guide Dog Training Centre is located at Cleve House, Exwick, one of five similar centres in the UK.

The Royal West of England School for the Deaf – is a non-maintained school funded mainly by local authorities. Of its 150 pupils of both sexes, all of whom have impaired hearing and some have additional handicaps, most come from the South West region. However, many pupils, particularly

those undertaking further education, come from a much wider area.

The school's modern buildings are set in 11 acres of grounds overlooking the River Exe. A combined teaching and care staff of 60 use computer technology along with traditional teaching methods, creating an atmosphere within which education and communication skills are developed. Teaching is organised at nursery, infant and primary levels, leading on to secondary, extended and further education.

A wide range of extra-curricular activities offer pupils a participating role in leisure and sport, both on site and outside the school.

The pictures show various activities undertaken in helping blind and deaf students.

FOCUS FOR THE REGION

SEMPER FIDELIS

121

O n the following pages a selected number of nationally important companies represent the 'focus for the region' aspect of Exeter's industrial and business base. Each company has different reasons for having chosen Exeter as a base for carrying out part or all of their activities, but all agree on one factor: the pleasing environment of the city.

Howmet (UK) Ltd – Located at Sowton, Howmet are one of the city's largest industrial employers. They are the leading UK manufacturers of precision cast airfoils for aero engines, used in most of the world's aircraft and industrial gas turbines. They also produce nickel and cobalt superalloys which play an essential role in high-tech industry.

Howmet (UK), Ltd are a subsidiary of the Howmet Corporation of America, a world leader in investment casting technology for over fifty years.

Exeter is a base for two modern facilities, employing approximately 900 people. A commitment to a continuous programme of recruitment and training of local people is maintained, while strong support from skilled and technical staff will always be a priority.

The photographs show the Howmet offices at Sowton, and various manufacturing processes.

Medical Sickness Group (comprising Medical Sickness Society and Permanent Insurance Company). Following a decision to relocate from Central London, the Group chose Exeter from over eighty towns considered from across the country. Quality of life, excellent schools, availability of good quality staff and housing and local amenities were principal among the deciding factors.

Some 35 per cent of the existing staff, including most of the executives and departmental heads and a large proportion of the computer and accounts sections, decided to make Devon their new home. In addition, the new headquarters have provided jobs for 200 local people.

The photographs show the splendid new Medical Sickness headquarters at Pynes Hill.

London & Manchester Assurance Company Ltd – Exeter is a carefully chosen location for the chief office of London and Manchester, the broadly-based UK financial services group. Easy access by road, rail and air, and the quality of life for its employees were two important factors in the relocation decision.

The attractive award-winning offices harmonize in style and scale with a handsome Georgian house, restored to its original splendour. The site also houses dining and recreation rooms, sports facilities and, seen as important by London & Manchester, a family centre aimed at bringing mothers back into business.

Light and open offices (inset) within a pleasing environment.

The delightful 80-acre parkland estate (above) at Winslade Park, Clyst St Mary, features lawns, woodland, sports fields and pastureland.

The splendid hall (left) of the Georgian house around which the new offices have been designed and built.

FOCUS FOR THE REGION

EBC Group plc – The EBC Group of Companies has developed over the last 52 years from 'Exeter Building Contractors', a company formed in 1939. EBC were involved in the rebuilding of the city following the blitz, and with many more significant buildings since that time.

EBC Group plc is a fully listed company operating as contractors, property developers and housebuilders throughout the South West region, with subsidiary offices in Bristol, Bournemouth, Torbay, Plymouth and Truro.

"Exeter is an excellent centre for our Head Office with its prime location on the M5. Devon is a fine place in which to live and do business and this is a considerable asset in attracting a quality team to run our affairs."

H. Cockroft,
Chairman and Chief Executive

Castle Square House, an EBC development in the city centre designed in collaboration with the City Council.

(Above, right) Curzon House, Southernhay East.

(Right) Retail development, High Street, Exeter – a prestigious EBC contract.

EBC Group Head Office, Cranmere Court, Lustleigh Close, Exeter.

National Mutual Life – National Mutual Property Services Ltd are responsible for the development of Southernhay Gardens. Office buildings are grouped around landscaped courtyards, linked by pedestrian routes. The scheme is a natural extension to the City's main office area in Southernhay, with a pedestrian walkway from the shopping centre through Cathedral Close.

Many important businesses are located in the scheme: Abbey Life Assurance Company; Abbey National Building Society; Bond Pearce; Cornhill Insurance; Equitable Life Assurance Company; Ford Simey Daw Roberts; Halifax Building Society; Hill Samuel Investment Services Group; KPMG Peat Marwick; Midland Bank; National Mutual Life Assurance Society; Save & Prosper; Sun Life Assurance Company.

FOCUS FOR THE REGION

SEMPER EADEM

Peninsula House.

NRA
National Rivers Authority
South West Region

MANLEY HOUSE

Roadford Lake.

National Rivers Authority – Set up in 1989 as the strongest environmental protection agency in Europe, the NRA's main responsibilities are for pollution control, flood defence, environmental monitoring, fisheries, recreation and conservation, and water resources planning and control. The South West Region headquarters of the NRA is at Sowton.

South West Water Plc has its headquarters at Peninsula House, Exeter. From this base the company controls water resources to millions of customers throughout the South West region. Massive schemes, such as the new Roadford reservoir, play a vital role in the lives of people throughout Devon.

The River Exe

University campus

Cathedral West Front

DevonAir

The Exeter Book is a celebration of the city past and present. It is a picture taken at a moment in time, revealing a city alive with history and vibrant with life.
Exeter will continue to change, just as it has undergone many changes since the Romans first built their walled fortress overlooking the River Exe. Exeter is an attractive and healthy place to live.
This is our heritage from which the future city will grow.

Radio Devon Newsroom

The Concorde at Exeter Airport

New offices, Express & Echo